LOVE GOD GREATLY
BIBLE
STORYBOOK

With Illustrations from
Children Around the World

Written by LOVE GOD GREATLY

Illustrated by Angie Alape Pérez

An Imprint of Thomas Nelson

Love God Greatly Bible Storybook

© 2025 Love God Greatly

Tommy Nelson, PO Box 141000, Nashville, TN 37214

Published in Nashville, Tennessee, by Tommy Nelson. Tommy Nelson is an imprint of Thomas Nelson. Thomas Nelson is a registered trademark of HarperCollins Christian Publishing, Inc.

Tommy Nelson titles may be purchased in bulk for educational, business, fund-raising, or sales promotional use. For information, please email SpecialMarkets@ThomasNelson.com.

ISBN 978-1-4002-4457-7 (audiobook)
ISBN 978-1-4002-4413-3 (eBook)
ISBN 978-1-4002-4445-4 (HC)

Library of Congress Cataloging-in-Publication

Names: Alape, Angie, illustrator. | Love God Greatly, author.
Title: Love God greatly Bible storybook : with illustrations from children around the world / written by Love God Greatly ; illustrated by Angie Alape Perez.
Description: Nashville, Tennessee, USA : Thomas Nelson, [2024] | Audience: Ages 5-11 | Summary: "With contributions from diverse voices and children around the world, the Love God Greatly Bible Storybook tells 40 Bible stories and shows how God's love stretches. By highlighting scriptural truth, global perspectives, and God's great love, kids will learn that the gift Jesus gave is for every person, in every country, from every culture"-- Provided by publisher.
Identifiers: LCCN 2024030864 | ISBN 9781400244454 (HC) | ISBN 9781400244577 (audiobook) | ISBN 9781400244133 (ePub)
Subjects: LCSH: Bible stories, English--Juvenile literature. | Bible--Illustrations--Juvenile literature.
Classification: LCC BS550.3 .L69 2024 | DDC 220.95/05--dc23/eng/20240719
LC record available at https://lccn.loc.gov/2024030864

Printed in Italy

25 26 27 28 29   ROT   5 4 3 2 1

Mfr: ROT / Pioltello, Italy / January 2025 / PO #12177218

We will tell the next generation about the
LORD'S praiseworthy acts, about his strength
and the amazing things he has done.

—Psalm 78:4

CONTENTS

INTRODUCTION

As a mom to three incredible daughters—Paige, Addie, and Brinnley—I've cherished the moments we've spent together reading Bible storybooks at bedtime. Those precious times of reading and discussing God's Word have nurtured their love for Jesus and laid the foundation for their understanding of who He is. It was in those early conversations that my children began to grasp the incredible character of God: His love, forgiveness, grace, and omniscience.

As a parent, introducing your children to Jesus and spending time together in His Word is the most valuable gift you can give them. While writing this Bible story-book, I prayed for you, your children, and the precious moments you'll share as you read these pages together. My heart's desire is that this book will help you and your little ones see how every story within these pages points to Jesus—the Rescuer our hearts long for and our souls need. I pray that, after reading this Bible storybook, both you and your children will find yourselves more in love with Jesus than when you began.

Before you start reading these narratives with your children, it is important for me to make clear that this is a storybook *about* the Bible. It is not *the* Bible, the inspired Word of God. Rather, it is an interpretative paraphrase of the Bible written for elementary school children, one that seeks to help them understand God's heart behind His words. Written as clearly and accurately as possible, this book aspires to show your children how they can see God's ultimate rescue mission throughout the pages of the Bible.

Two features make this Bible storybook so special. One is the Thoughts from Around the World section at the end of each story, written by women from all over the globe. These notes, written to your family about the story you've just read, will remind you that believers everywhere are connected by these truths. The second is its beautiful use of artwork and prayers contributed by children from all over the world. By admiring their artwork and reading their prayers, you and your children can catch a glimpse of the beauty of the global body of Christ and how Jesus is reaching the hearts and lives of children across the globe.

Jesus truly does love the little children, all the children of the world.

Angela from Love God Greatly

A LETTER TO KIDS

Jesus loves you. Above all else, I want you to know that. Every story you are about to read points back to Jesus and the incredible rescue mission He is on. It is important to know that the stories you are about to read are not fantasy stories; they are real, and they happened. Remember, God is loving, full of grace, forgiving, and holy. He knows everything about us: the good, the bad, and the ugly. Yes, He knows it all, and He still chooses to love us. He's the best friend you could ever dream of and hope to have, except He isn't a dream. He is real, He is alive, and He loves you. You are important to Him—so important that He willingly and obediently died on the cross for your sins and mine. That just shows you how important you are to Him . . . but I don't want to get too far ahead of myself. You will learn more about this amazing rescue mission as you read this Bible storybook.

As you read this book with your family, my prayer is that each of you will love Jesus more than when you started reading. And when you reach the final page, I pray that you will choose to love God greatly with the precious life He has given you and help other children learn about Jesus and how much He loves them too.

And guess what? You are about to meet some pretty incredible kids from all over the world! You will see their artwork and read their prayers. How awesome is that? I can't wait for you to get started!

Angela from Love God Greatly

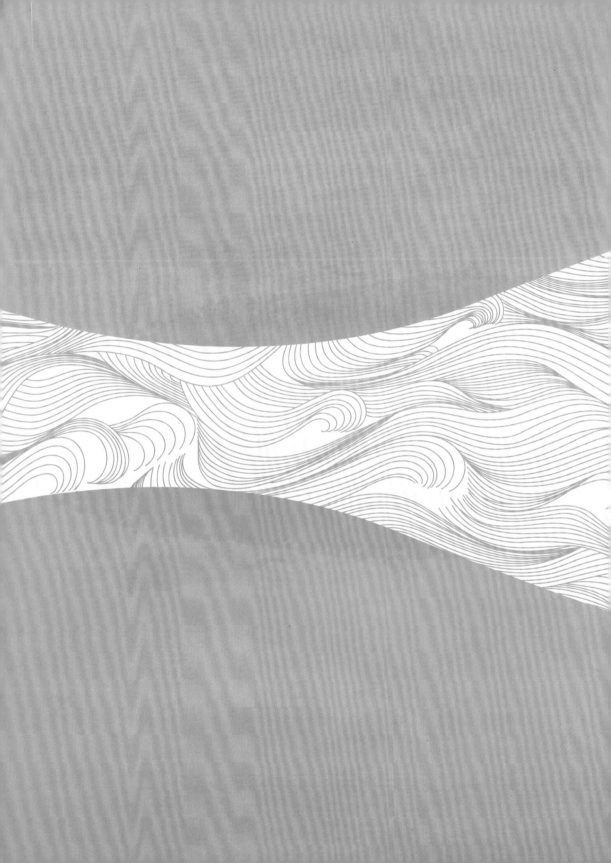

OLD
TESTAMENT

01

CREATION

From the beginning of all beginnings, God was there. In the beginning, there was only God. In the dark nothingness that first existed, God was there. And out of the nothingness, God created. He is the Creator of all things. God has always existed and always will.

Our world and everything in it was not created by accident. It was created for a purpose. God created because He wanted to, not because He needed to or because He was missing something. God chose to create our world because He is love, and what He creates is an expression of His love.

And so, with eyes full of love, God looked at the dark nothingness and spoke. "Let there be light."

God's words are powerful. When God spoke, light burst forth out of the nothingness. Since that moment, light has always overcome darkness. And God called the light *day* and the darkness *night*. So the first day came to a close.

On the second day, God spoke and created the beautiful blue sky.

On the third day, God spoke, and land appeared from the deep waters. On the land, God created plants with seeds and trees with fruit. **All of them were created out of love for what was to come.**

On the fourth day, God spoke again, and with a twinkle in His eyes, He put the sun, moon, and sparkling stars in place. He made them as a forever reminder in the sky that, no matter day or night, God is near.

On the fifth day, God filled the waters with different types of fish and other kinds of exciting water creatures. Then, He filled the skies with birds. Some He made small, others He made large, but each one He made beautiful in its own way. But God *still* wasn't done creating.

On the sixth day, God created the land animals. He made short ones and tall ones, big ones and small ones. Tigers and lions and monkeys galore. But you know what? **God saved the most special part of His creation for the very end.** Everything He had made so far was leading up to this final, incredible masterpiece. And so, with love in His heart, God made people, both male and female. And when He looked at them, His eyes were full of love, just like a proud daddy looking at his children for the first time. God's heart was bursting with joy, not because of anything His children had done, but simply because they were His. From His life, He gave them life, as it would always be.

On the seventh day, God rested. Not because He needed to, but because He wanted to. God rested to pause and enjoy everything He had created. And as He looked around, He rejoiced because it was all good—*very* good. The universe, the heavens, the earth, and everything on and in the earth was very good, and God delighted in His creation.

Thank You, Lord, for creating the big things and the small things. Thank You for making people in Your own image for Your glory, and thank You for Your love that never ends. Amen.

Prayer by Elias | FROM POLAND AND CANADA

Thoughts from Around the World

Do you like to make things? One of my kids likes building things out of LEGOs, and another has started carving things out of wood. It is amazing to see the things they create! When they are done creating, something is there that wasn't there before. This is like what God did when He created the world! He spoke, and by the power of His words, He created *everything*! The mountains and the seas, the tiny ant and the huge elephant. And then He made humans—a man and a woman—in His image. It is because we are made in His image that we are also creators! While we can't literally create something out of nothing, God wants us to use our creativity to worship Him and bring Him glory!

Written by Krista | FROM POLAND AND CANADA

THE GARDEN OF EDEN

God created the first man, Adam, and gave him a beautiful garden to live in called Eden. Eden was the most beautiful garden that has ever existed, beyond anything we could imagine. God filled the garden of Eden with plants, trees, and animals for Adam to delight in and take care of. But God noticed that it was not good for Adam to be alone. So God created a woman, Eve, to complement him and help him. Together, Adam and Eve tended to the beautiful garden God had lovingly placed them in. By taking care of the garden God had given to them, Adam and Eve honored Him with their work.

Now, of all the things God created, Adam and Eve were the most special. Why? Because they were created in His image. They were created to reflect God. Unlike all the animals, Adam and Eve were made to have a relationship with God, as well as relationships with each other. When God looked upon them, His heart filled with love. He enjoyed the relationship He had with both of them, as God would walk with them in the garden of Eden.

In the middle of this perfect garden stood two trees. One tree was called the Tree of Life, and the other was called the Tree of the Knowledge of Good and Evil. God gave one rule to Adam and Eve that would keep them safe. God told them that they could eat from any tree in the whole garden except the Tree of the Knowledge of Good and Evil. Why did God do this? It was because if Adam and Eve ate the fruit of the forbidden tree and disobeyed God's one rule, it would lead to pain, sadness, and death. This act of disobedience would also hurt Adam and Eve's ability to have a close relationship with God and each other.

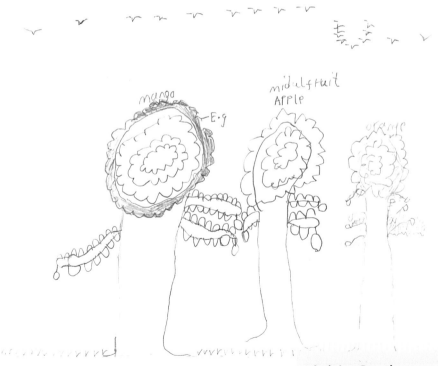

Art by Ben | FROM KENYA

Adam and Eve had a choice, just like you and I do. They could choose to obey God and trust that He loved them and knew what was best for them, or they could choose not to trust God and disobey Him. One of the many gifts that God gives all of us is called *free will*. That means each of us is free to choose to obey God or disobey Him. God wants a personal relationship with us, but He will not force it. He loves us regardless of whether we love Him back, but He desires for us to "walk and talk" with Him, just like Adam and Eve did at one time. Adam and Eve were made for a relationship with God, and so are we.

Thank You, Lord, for giving us Your Son, Jesus Christ. In Him we have confidence of our salvation. Amen.

Prayer by Ben | FROM KENYA

Thoughts from Around the World

Unlike my city, Nairobi, which is full of buildings and cars, God created Adam and Eve in a peaceful and awesome garden full of trees and animals. They were created in the image and likeness of God.

God created them to have a relationship with Him. God wants to have a relationship with us too.

Written by Gail | FROM KENYA

03

THE FALL

GENESIS 3

Now, somebody else was inside the beautiful garden of Eden with Adam and Eve: Satan, who was disguised as a sneaky serpent. Satan hated God and wanted Adam and Eve to hate God too. At one time, Satan had been the most beautiful angel in heaven. But over time, he had grown prideful. He no longer wanted just to be a beautiful angel; he wanted to be *God*, and he wanted to be worshiped. Just as God is all good, Satan is all evil. There is nothing evil in God, and there is nothing good in Satan. Satan is God's enemy, but he is not God's equal.

And so, disguised as a serpent, Satan went to tempt Eve. And as he has done with every person after her, Satan made Eve question if God really loved her and wanted the best for her life. The way he did this was *really* sneaky: Satan took God's one and only rule and twisted it.

"Did God really say you can't eat from *any* tree in the garden?" he asked.

"We can eat from the trees," Eve explained, "except for one tree in the middle of the garden. God said, 'Do not eat from it or even touch it. If you do, then you will die.'"

"But you won't die!" Satan the serpent said. "God knows as soon as you eat it, you'll be just like *Him*. You'll know things the way He does, like what's good and what's evil."

And there, Eve was tempted with a choice. Did she trust God and believe He only wanted good for her, or did she think God was holding back good things from her? For the first time ever, Eve doubted that God really wanted the best for her life. For the first time ever, Eve thought she could be as wise as God.

With doubt in her heart, Eve took a bite of the forbidden fruit from the forbidden tree. Adam ate the fruit too, even though he also knew the one and only rule God had given them was not to eat from that tree.

And at that moment, the world went from a perfect one to a broken one. Adam and Eve's choice to believe the serpent's lie and not trust God's love for them brought sin, pain, sadness, and brokenness for them and everyone else after them.

After Adam and Eve ate the forbidden fruit, they felt a new emotion they hadn't before: they felt *shame*. And it didn't feel good. We feel shame when we have made a mistake or don't feel like we measure up in some way. In the garden Adam and Eve felt shame because they realized they were naked. The shame made them feel bad

Art by Helena | FROM BRAZIL

about themselves, so they tried to fix their nakedness on their own, without God's help. They knew they had disobeyed God, so when Adam and Eve heard God walking in the garden, instead of running to Him with joy and love in their hearts, they hid from Him. Sin has a way of making people feel they need to hide from God.

"Where are you?" God called out to Adam and Eve.

"We are hiding because we are naked," Adam replied.

God already knew what they had done, and His heart broke. "Who told you that you were naked? Did you disobey Me and eat the fruit from the one and only tree I told you not to?" God then made clothes for Adam and Eve to cover their nakedness.

God knew that from this moment on, His relationship with His children would be different. Sin had entered the world, and it would never be the same. Though God had made them to live forever, Adam and Eve would now have to face death.

Though God was heartbroken because of Adam and Eve's decision to disobey Him, God's love for them was stronger than the pain He felt. **God would fix the brokenness that had entered the world.**

Even though Adam and Eve would have to suffer the consequences of their disobedience and no longer live in the beautiful garden of Eden, God would also reveal to them that no matter how much they hurt Him, He would never stop loving them. Yes, sin broke their relationship, but God would make a way to repair it. The brokenness in the world would not last forever.

In a way that only God could do, He would fix all the pain, suffering, and sin that entered the world through Adam and Eve's sin. Sin would not have the final say in what would happen to God's creation—God would. He would do this by laying down His only Son's life as our perfect Rescuer to defeat sin once and for all.

Remember, nothing in this world is more powerful than God.

Heavenly Father, help me to obey and honor Your Holy Word, my parents, my teachers, and those who take care of me. Thank You for Your faithfulness and for always guiding me to the truth. Help me to stay away from everything that distances me from You. In Jesus' name, amen.

Prayer by Helena | FROM BRAZIL

Thoughts from Around the World

"You can play outside only after you finish all your homework!" Is this phrase familiar to you? Are you one of those children who immediately obeys their parents, or do you have fun before doing what you've been told to do? In this story, the serpent lied so that Adam and Eve would disobey the rule that God had given them. Can you see how Adam and Eve's disobedience brought pain and suffering? From this story I learned that God is faithful to what He says and that Satan lies. Disobedience leads to death, but obedience leads to life.

Written by Giovanna | FROM BRAZIL

04

NOAH AND THE FLOOD

GENESIS 6:1–9:17

After Adam and Eve were told to leave the garden of Eden, they had children, and their children had children. The earth filled with people, and eventually, after many, many years, everyone forgot about God. They forgot that Adam and Eve used to know God and walk with Him. They started living only for their selfish interests and doing very bad things. The earth became full of violence, and God knew He had to do something to stop it.

But in this violent and evil world, one man and his family still knew God and loved Him. That man's name was Noah, and Noah loved God very much. Even when those around him didn't love God, Noah did. Noah cared more about what God thought of him than what others thought of him. And that was a very good decision to make, because choosing to love God and live for His approval instead of the approval of those around Noah was worth it. And because Noah had a relationship with God, God spoke to him.

One day, God told Noah that He was so sad with how violent and evil the world had become that He would have to step in and stop it. He was going to flood the earth and start over. There was no longer anyone in the world who loved and obeyed God except Noah and his family.

Art by Ava | FROM THE UNITED STATES OF AMERICA

So God decided to do something very special through Noah and his family, because Noah loved God. God told Noah to build a *really* big boat called an ark out in the middle of nowhere, far away from any body of water! I know, it sounds crazy! Noah may not have understood why God wanted him to build the ark, but he trusted God even when it didn't make sense.

So Noah built the ark. God gave Noah very specific instructions on how to build the ark, because this special boat was going to serve a very special purpose. A storm was coming, and God would use this ark to protect this special family.

If building a boat in the middle of nowhere weren't crazy enough, God told Noah that the ark had to be big enough to be filled with animals, like a big floating zoo! God would send two of every kind of animal, one male and one female, for Noah and his family to take care of on the ark.

After a long time, Noah finally finished building the ark, just as God had instructed him. The time came for God to fill the ark with all the animals. Big animals and little animals, tall animals and small animals—they all started making their way to the ark. And once everyone was safe inside, God shut the door.

Once the door of the ark shut, the storm came, just as God had said would happen. At first, it was just a few raindrops, but those raindrops turned into a downpour, and the downpour turned into the biggest storm the world would ever see. The storm lasted for forty days and forty nights.

By the time the storm was over, the whole world was covered in water. Even the tallest of tall mountains were covered in water. But God was still with Noah and his family. God protected them in the storm, just as He had promised. And Noah learned that what God promises, He fulfills.

After the rain finally stopped, the water started to recede, and dry land began to appear. Once it was safe, God opened the ark door, and Noah, his family, and all the animals came out. But God had one more special surprise left for Noah and his family—a promise to never flood the whole earth again. Up in the sky, God placed the most beautiful rainbow. God did this so that every time Noah, his children, and his children's children would see the rainbow, they would be reminded of God's special promise.

God was starting the world all over again. Noah's sons had children, and those children grew up and had children of their own. This continued for some time until the earth was filled with people once more. Even though Noah and his family had a relationship with God, they were still sinners. Remember, Adam and Eve's sinful nature was passed down to every human. This is why the people who came after

Noah and his family began living for themselves again. They forgot how God had protected Noah and his family from the great flood. People stopped loving God, but God had another plan. Sin would one day be washed away again, but not by water from a big storm. No, the next time, sin would be washed away by a loving Savior.

God, please help me to be faithful to You like Noah was. Help me to listen to You, even if other people do not. Amen.

Prayer by Ava | FROM THE UNITED STATES OF AMERICA

Thoughts from Around the World

Noah and his family were different. They stood out. The people around them had forgotten about God, but Noah chose to listen to God and follow what He said to do. His neighbors probably thought he was crazy to be building a huge boat in the middle of nowhere, but he didn't care how it looked. He led his family with his faithfulness to God, and God protected Noah and his family when the rain came.

It's okay to not look like the rest of the world. God called us to be different. He made you to be you and me to be me, and He calls us all to follow Him, no matter what others are doing or saying. When we do that, we can know that He will show us the right way to go.

Written by Rachel | FROM THE UNITED STATES OF AMERICA

05

ABRAHAM AND THE COVENANT

Many years passed since the earth was flooded, and Noah's family grew and grew. But the same thing happened again as more and more people filled the earth: they continued sinning. They stopped loving and obeying God. Once again, violence and evil returned to the world. God had promised Noah He wouldn't send another flood, so this time God decided to help His children through another good man and his family.

This man's name was Abraham. Abraham loved God, just like Noah did. But Abraham was sad because he didn't have any children.

One day God went to Abraham and told him to trust Him. Then, God had Abraham look up into the night sky that was filled with twinkling stars. God told Abraham to count the stars, but Abraham couldn't—there were just too many of them! Then God promised Abraham that someday He was going to give Abraham his heart's desire—Abraham was going to have more family members than the number of stars in the night sky!

"One day," God told Abraham, "you will have a great family of your own. And your family will be very special to Me."

Art by Nathaniel | FROM GREECE

Abraham didn't know how that would be possible, since he didn't have any children yet and he was already very old. Abraham's wife, Sarah, was old too. **But Abraham believed God's generous promise, and that made God very happy.**

Like Noah, Abraham didn't know how God would do what He said He would do, but Abraham chose to trust God anyway. He trusted God because Abraham knew God was good, kind, and gracious. What we think about God is very important, because it impacts how much we trust God when things in our lives don't make sense.

That night, God made a covenant with Abraham. A *covenant* is a special, unbreakable contract or promise. God knew the people in the world were turning away from Him again, but this time God was going to bless the world through Abraham's special family. Through this family that God set apart from everyone else, God would send the much-needed Rescuer to come and save the world from sin. Through this special family, the world would be blessed.

Dear God, thank You for being next to me and for guiding and guarding my every step. I am praying for You to give me courage to be different and show the impact of Your presence in my life. Amen.

Prayer by Nathaniel | FROM GREECE

Thoughts from Around the World

God uses us in ways we may not understand. We may feel that it is impossible for us to achieve something. But with God's help and guidance, nothing is impossible, no matter how difficult it may seem. God is always near to those who love Him and trust Him. He can hear our prayers, and He knows what our hearts desire.

It is okay to be different from those around us. We can trust God and seek guidance from Him. We can rely on God for everything because He can do everything in His strength. We need to have patience and continue trusting and believing in God's promises, no matter what. God is always with us, and He cares about us. We can trust Him!

Written by Irene | FROM GREECE

06

THE BIRTH OF ISAAC

GENESIS 18:1–15; 21:1–8

One of the most wonderful things about God is that He keeps His promises. God never has and never will break a promise He has made. He is the ultimate promise keeper!

When God promised Abraham that one day he would have a family of his own, God kept that promise. What seemed impossible to Abraham, his wife Sarah, and all their friends, God made possible. It is important to always remember that absolutely nothing is impossible for God. Like Abraham, we must choose to trust God, even when we don't understand His plan.

Now Abraham's wife, Sarah, had to learn that lesson the hard way. When she heard God's promise that she would give birth to a child the next year, she laughed. She laughed because the idea seemed impossible.

Like Abraham, Sarah desperately wanted a family of her own. At this time, Sarah was already very old. She had prayed and waited many years for God to bless her with a child, but He hadn't yet. By now she felt her dream of being a mother was too far gone and that she was too old to have a baby. So Sarah laughed when she heard the news to keep herself from crying. Her heart desperately wanted to believe God's promise, but her mind thought it was impossible.

Art by Mája | FROM THE CZECH REPUBLIC

And yet, just as God had said would happen, nine months later the cry of a new-born baby boy rang out in Abraham and Sarah's house. Abraham and Sarah both cried when the baby was born, but their tears were not sad tears but rather tears of joy! God had kept His promise! What seemed impossible to them was possible for God.

Abraham and Sarah named this long-awaited baby Isaac, which means "laughter." Because after waiting so many years, God had answered Abraham and Sarah's prayers and kept His promise. Laughter would now fill their hearts and home.

Dear Lord, even when everything seems to go the wrong way, I know that You can change it. Please help me trust in You. Amen.

Prayer by Mája | FROM THE CZECH REPUBLIC

Thoughts from Around the World

Have you ever made a promise? Maybe you've promised to tidy your room, eat all of your dinner, or do your homework. These are all great promises. But I'm sure, like me, there have been times where you have broken one of these promises. God, however, never breaks His promises. The story of Abraham, Sarah, and baby Isaac is just one of the many examples in the Bible where God kept His promise. We can always trust Him, even when we think something is impossible. The Bible tells us that God cannot lie. This is amazing news for you and me! As you enjoy this day, know that God is with you, and He always keeps His promises.

Written by Petra | FROM THE CZECH REPUBLIC

07

JOSEPH AND HIS BROTHERS

GENESIS 37

D o you remember how God promised Abraham that one day he would have a very large family? **Well, as we know, God always keeps His promises.** Abraham's son Isaac was the father of two sons. One of his sons, named Jacob, grew up and had twelve sons of his own! Now that's a big family!

Isaac's son Jacob loved all his children, but one son was especially dear to his heart. (God doesn't have favorites, but unfortunately, Jacob did.) Jacob loved his son Joseph more than all his other boys. This not only hurt his other sons' feelings, but it also made them jealous of their brother. Joseph may have been their dad's favorite, but he was not *their* favorite.

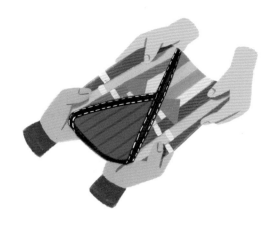

One day, Jacob gave his son Joseph a very special gift. It was a beautiful robe made of many different colors. Not only was it an amazing gift, but none of the other brothers got one. This hurt all their feelings and made them dislike Joseph so much that they hated him.

To make matters worse, Joseph began having some interesting dreams. In one of his dreams, Joseph saw the sun, moon, and eleven stars bowing down to him. Joseph's brothers didn't like this dream. It sounded like Joseph thought their entire family, including the brothers, would one day bow down to him. Joseph's brothers became very angry with him. They said they would never bow down to this little brother of theirs!

Art by Zoé | FROM THE NETHERLANDS

As Joseph grew, so did the hatred his brothers had for him. One day Joseph's dad sent him on an errand to check in on his brothers, who were working in the pasture of a nearby town. When the brothers saw Joseph coming, they knew they finally had a chance to get rid of their spoiled sibling. They grabbed Joseph and tore off the special robe their father had given him. They threw him into a deep, dark hole, and then, when slave traders came by, they sold him for twenty pieces of silver. How cruel! The slave traders then took Joseph far away to the land of Egypt.

Once they were back home, Joseph's brothers tricked their dad, Jacob. They tore up Joseph's beautiful robe and covered it with animal blood to make it look like their brother had been eaten by a wild animal. Jacob was heartbroken.

Betrayed by his brothers, sold into slavery, and sent to a foreign land far from his father's love, Joseph felt alone. **And yet, God was with Joseph.** Even when bad things happened to him, God was still with Joseph. It's the same for you and me. You may not always feel like God is with you, especially when you are going through a hard time. But God is always with you. On your best days and worst days, God is always by your side and working everything out for your good. God is so powerful that He can even bring good out of the bad things that happen to you, as you'll see later in Joseph's story.

Lord God, You are mighty and wonderful. You can give dreams to people and help them understand them. You are so great. Amen.

Prayer by Zoé | FROM THE NETHERLANDS

Thoughts from Around the World

I grew up in a large family, just like Joseph's. We had many quarrels about who was the smartest, the biggest, and the funniest. I never got the feeling that my father loved me or one of my siblings more than the others, but I can imagine that must have been very hard for the brothers of Joseph, especially when their younger brother dreamed about being the most important one. I am the oldest. Growing up, I always wanted to be the one my siblings respected. I can imagine why Joseph's older brothers got so angry and upset with him.

Do you ever feel upset with your brother or sister, or maybe with a friend? What do you do when you get angry with them? Maybe you say something mean or hurtful. Maybe you make them feel sad or upset. In the story of Joseph, God was with Joseph, but He was also with his brothers. As you'll see, God gave Joseph's brothers an opportunity to make things right with him. It is never too late to say that you're sorry when you hurt someone. God wants us to forgive each other and make things right.

Written by Charissa | FROM THE NETHERLANDS

08

JOSEPH RECONCILES WITH HIS BROTHERS

While he was enslaved in Egypt, Joseph worked really hard. Potiphar, the man who owned Joseph, noticed how hard he worked. Potiphar gave Joseph more and more responsibility until, eventually, he was put in charge of everything that Potiphar owned! That was a huge honor! Then one day, someone told a lie about Joseph and blamed him for something he didn't do. Even though Joseph was innocent, he was still punished and thrown in jail. I'm sure Joseph must have been really sad, especially since things in his life were finally starting to go well.

But even in jail, God was with Joseph. First, God gave Joseph favor with the main guard who was in charge of the jail. Soon, Joseph found himself in charge of the whole jail! Whatever work Joseph did, God blessed it, and those in charge of him noticed.

Then, a worker from the royal palace was put in jail with Joseph, and he had a dream that he didn't understand. He told Joseph about his dream, and God gave Joseph the ability to interpret it and tell the worker what it meant. Joseph asked the man to put in a good word for him with the king of Egypt, known as Pharaoh, when he was set free, but the man forgot!

Then one night Pharaoh had a dream too. His dream was about seven skinny cows and seven fat cows. Pharaoh couldn't figure out what the dream meant, and none of his advisors could either. But the palace worker Joseph had helped in jail finally remembered how Joseph had interpreted his dream, and he told Pharaoh about Joseph. Pharaoh sent for Joseph to explain the meaning of his dream. And once again, God gave Joseph the ability to interpret the dream.

Joseph explained to Pharaoh that his dream showed there were going to be seven years of lots of food but then seven years of famine when people would be hungry. Joseph advised Pharaoh to plan for the coming famine so his people would have enough food. Pharaoh was so impressed with Joseph and his wisdom that he freed Joseph from jail and made him the second most powerful ruler of Egypt! Joseph may have felt unseen in the jail, but God used him there.

For seven years, Joseph worked hard to store up all the extra food they grew. He was getting ready for the seven years of famine that were coming. And when those seven years of famine hit, they were really tough. People in other places were so hungry because they didn't have any food. But the people in Egypt? They had plenty to eat, all thanks to Joseph and the amazing skills God gave him to be a great leader! Because of this, lots of people from other countries came to Egypt to buy food during the famine.

Then one day, Joseph had a big surprise! A group of men from Canaan came to see him to buy food for their families. Although they didn't recognize him, Joseph knew immediately who they were. These men were *his brothers*! As they bowed down to him, Joseph remembered the dream he had when he was a young boy. Tears filled his eyes, and he knew he had a choice to make. Would he forgive his brothers and help them, or would he punish them for what they had done to him? Joseph prayed and asked God for help. Then he remembered how even in the bad times, God was always with him. He knew God had placed him in this powerful position so that he could help not only strangers but also his brothers in their time of need. Instead of revenge, Joseph chose to forgive his brothers and help them.

Joseph's brothers were shocked when they found out that this powerful man who was in charge of Egypt was actually their brother, the boy they had been mean to and sold into slavery all those years ago. At first, they were afraid that Joseph would punish them for how they had treated him. But then Joseph did the unexpected: he offered forgiveness instead of punishment and love instead of hate. Instead of punishing his brothers for selling him into slavery, he chose to give them food for their starving families and freedom from their guilt.

Many years later, in a different country but out of the same family, God would send another Rescuer to help starving people. This time these people weren't starving for food but starving for forgiveness for their sins.

God, help me be as loving and forgiving as Joseph was. Amen.

Prayer by Amanda | FROM HUNGARY

Thoughts from Around the World

Just like Joseph, I grew up in a big family. It is great to have a big family, but it's not always easy to have loving relationships with each other. I don't know about you, but we had some pretty bad fights when we were little kids. Sometimes when one of us got hurt, we would try to pay back the sibling who hurt us. There is a lesson in Joseph's story that encourages us to act differently!

Joseph's life was not dependent on his brothers' bad decisions or determined by the lie he was accused of. His life was led and blessed by God, no matter where he was—even in prison. God used Joseph mightily to save many people's lives during the famine. My favorite part of the story is how God shows that He cares about our relationships and hearts too, not just that we would be fed. When the brothers came to buy food, God gave them the chance to show their changed hearts, and He helped Joseph to forgive them instead of taking revenge.

My siblings and I had to learn to forgive each other, and we are best friends today! Jesus is always with you and helps you to forgive people who have wronged you. He gives you opportunities to shine for Him right where you are, just like Joseph!

Written by Viola | FROM HUNGARY

09

GENESIS 46-47; EXODUS 1-12

As the famine in Egypt continued, Joseph's family moved to Egypt so they would have enough food to eat. After a while they decided to stay in Egypt and raise their families. Over the years, Joseph's family grew and grew until there were thousands of them. Life was good when Joseph was alive, but things began to change after Joseph died and a new pharaoh, one who didn't know Joseph, was put in charge. When this new pharaoh saw how big and powerful Joseph's family was becoming, he began to worry they could eventually take over Egypt. So he decided to enslave God's people. You see, when people stop valuing each other and seeing one another as equal and made in the image of God, hatred can fill their hearts and lead them to do very unkind things to each other. **We must always remember that all people are made in the image of God, and therefore no one is more valuable than another.**

This new pharaoh was cruel. He made Joseph's family work very, very hard as enslaved people in his land. As the years passed and the cruelty continued, Joseph's family began to cry out to God for help. They needed someone to free them from this harsh land of slavery. So they prayed, asking God for help. And you know what? God heard each and every one of their prayers. He had not forgotten the promise He made to Abraham. What God promises He always fulfills. And as His people prayed, God's plan of deliverance was already in motion.

In the midst of their suffering, God raised up a deliverer named Moses. He was chosen to be the answer to their fervent prayers, the one who would lead them out of the chains of slavery and into freedom. Moses had to put his complete trust in God, even when it meant risking his own life.

One day, God spoke to Moses and told him to go to Pharaoh and tell him to let His people go. Moses was afraid to do this. Pharaoh was mean and cruel, and Moses did not like talking in front of people. But God told Moses not to be afraid but to trust Him. God reminded Moses that He would be with him. So Moses obeyed God and confronted the cruel pharaoh. Moses told Pharaoh that the way he was treating Joseph's family, the Israelites, was wrong. It was time for the Israelites to go back home to Canaan, the land God had promised His people, where their ancestors Abraham, Isaac, and Jacob had lived.

But Pharaoh refused to let the Israelites leave.

So God sent ten punishments called *plagues* to the people in Egypt, to show Pharaoh that He was serious. God turned water into blood. He sent gross frogs, annoying gnats, and swarming flies. He caused the livestock to be sick and boils to appear on the Egyptians and their animals. God sent hail, hungry grasshoppers, and a deep darkness that covered the land.

God sent these plagues to show that He wanted His people freed. But Pharaoh didn't know God or love God, so he didn't care what God wanted. His heart was so hard that he didn't care how much his own people suffered. He still refused to let the Israelites go . . . until the last plague.

God told Moses to tell each Israelite family to pick their most perfect and flawless lamb. They would need to kill it and put some of the lamb's blood on their front doors. This would protect their house from the final plague that was coming.

That night, *all* the firstborn sons of all the families in Egypt died, including Pharaoh's son. But the firstborn sons of the Israelites did not die—the perfect and flawless lamb died in the place of their firstborn sons.

As you can imagine, there was a lot of crying in Egypt. Pharaoh's heart was broken. He hadn't listened to God and *all* the warnings God had given him through Moses. Pharaoh's stubbornness and unwillingness to obey God cost him his son's life.

Pharaoh cried tears of sorrow and pain. Finally in his heartache and anger, Pharaoh told Moses and his brother, Aaron, to take the Israelites and go. Young and old, short and tall, the Israelites took their possessions and left Egypt. After years of slavery, they were free.

Art by Natalie | FROM THE UNITED STATES OF AMERICA AND JAPAN

God never wanted the Israelites to forget the night He rescued His people and forced Pharaoh to let His people go. This night was called Passover because during that final plague God "passed over" all the houses that had the blood of the lamb on their doors. But this Passover night was just a foreshadowing of a greater rescue mission. An even greater deliverance was still coming.

Jesus, thank You for protecting Your people. Amen.

Prayer by Natalie | FROM THE UNITED STATES OF AMERICA AND JAPAN

Thoughts from Around the World

God is always with us. He always hears us and guides us. He heard the Israelites' prayers, and He guided them and provided for them. God made a way for us to be saved, just like the Israelites. He brought us someone to guide us, protect us, and lead us. Jesus Christ is our great Shepherd, our Leader, and our Guide. And He's also the Lamb of God, a sacrifice for us.

Just like the lambs in the Passover story, Jesus' blood saves us. Because of Jesus, we are always covered by His love and protection. Even when we forget what God has done, God is still here, and He will always hear our prayers. We don't need to fear. We can always trust and know He is there.

Written by Vicky | FROM THE UNITED STATES OF AMERICA AND THAILAND

10

EXODUS 13–15

Affter years of praying and waiting, Abraham's promised family and God's chosen people were finally free!

The Israelites were so excited to leave Egypt, their land of slavery, that first Passover night! And God was gracious and good to them. He visibly showed He was with them as He led them out of Egypt. By day, God led them as a pillar of cloud, showing them the direction to go. By night, God was a pillar of fire, His light helping them travel even in the darkness. And life was good . . . until it wasn't.

At first, the people heard a faint rumble in the distance and saw a speck of something on the horizon. But as the Israelites looked back toward Egypt, back toward their land of slavery, fear rushed into their hearts. Pharaoh had changed his mind yet again, and he and his army were coming after them! In that moment, a mix of fear and what-ifs began to take root in their minds and hearts. God's chosen people began to doubt His goodness, even though He had just miraculously rescued them. "Did God bring us out here just to have us killed?" they asked. They found themselves tempted to go back. Back to the cruel land they knew instead of walking forward, free into an unfamiliar land and an uncertain future. "Maybe life in Egypt wasn't as bad as we thought!" Yes, they were free, but at what cost? Would they just die here in the desert?

The Israelites found themselves trapped between the Red Sea in front of them and an army of angry Egyptians behind them. They didn't sign up for this. They cried and complained to God. *Why has God done this to us?* they wondered. Regret and fear overtook them sooner than the Egyptian chariots ever could. In their moment of fear, they forgot all the miracles God had just done.

Fear has a way of poisoning our memories and making us doubt God.

Now the Israelites had a choice. They could trust God to rescue them once again, even though it seemed impossible, or surrender and go back to Egypt to be enslaved. But crossing the Red Sea seemed impossible. They didn't have boats, and it was too far for them to swim across and too deep for them to walk across.

Just then Moses' voice rang out, "Do not fear! God will fight this battle for you!" And He did.

God sent a strong wind that was so powerful that it split the sea in two! The water rose up and formed two tall walls, one on the right and one on the left, and the Israelites walked across on dry ground safely to the other side. As the Egyptians in their chariots closed in and began to cross the Red Sea, God stopped the wind and closed the sea back up. All the water from the sea came crashing down on the Egyptians. Not one of them survived!

Art by Richard | FROM UGANDA

Once again, God saved His precious children! But this wouldn't be the last time they would need His help. In the future, the Israelites would find themselves in many more scary situations where they would forget about the goodness of God and how He had rescued them in the past. Yet God would remember the Israelites, and He would step in and save them.

But there was a day coming, many years later, when God would rescue His people once and for all—not from the slavery of human hands but from the slavery of sin.

Dear Lord, I pray children in my country know You. May they receive clothes, food, and education. May they not fear, for You are with them. I pray they receive peace and know that You are right by their side. Amen.

Prayer by Richard | FROM UGANDA

Thoughts from Around the World

As a Christian living in Uganda, I read the story of the Israelites crossing the sea as a story of hope. Many of our people here live on the promises of God every day. This story gives us hope as we wait for God's redemption from the chains of the enemy. Many of us here experience struggles, poverty, and persecution. But this story creates a ray of hope, for it says we should never give up, no matter the situation. The Israelites were full of anxiety before they were able to cross the sea. But then God made His power known by dividing the sea. He created a dry passage for His chosen people, and He destroyed their enemy right before their eyes.

Since we live in a community with limited access to Christian teaching or materials, we long to learn more about God's Word. Discovering that the miraculous crossing of the sea took place on African soil fills our hearts with pride. It's incredibly encouraging to know that God chose our continent as the stage for His mighty act of deliverance, rescuing His people right here in Africa!

Written by Sylvia | FROM UGANDA

11

THE TEN COMMANDMENTS

EXODUS 16–17, 19–20

After being rescued by God at the Red Sea, Moses led the Israelites into the wilderness. As the people walked and walked, their feet began to hurt, their tummies began to rumble, and they started to complain. Why did they have to take such a hard route to the Promised Land? It seemed to them that if Moses were really leading them to where God wanted, the route would be much easier.

God heard their complaining, and again He answered by giving the Israelites just what they needed. God sent them special food called *manna*. It literally rained down from heaven for the people to eat each day! God also gave them clean water that burst out of a rock. **God was showing His chosen people not only how powerful He is but also that they could trust Him to meet their needs.**

And yet, even after those miracles, the Israelites *still* struggled to trust God and remember all He had done for them. They still found themselves doubting God's love and protection again and again, always wondering if there were someone or something else who would be better to follow.

Then one day, God told Moses He wanted to talk to His chosen people. He wanted them to know that He loved them and wanted them to get to know Him better too. He wanted them to know that they had a pretty incredible mission. God's chosen people were to reflect Him to the world and help others know God as well. To do that, God gave Moses ten special rules, known as the Ten Commandments, for the people to follow.

Of all the Ten Commandments, the most important one was to love God more than anything else in the world. Why? Because God knew that if the Israelites loved someone or something else more than Him, they would end up getting hurt. God loved His chosen people so much and wanted to protect them from unnecessary pain.

The other commandments instructed the Israelites not to have idols or take the Lord's name in vain, and they were to keep the Sabbath day holy. God commanded them to honor their parents and to never murder, commit adultery, steal, lie, or be jealous of what other people had. While these rules might not seem so hard to keep, God's chosen people kept disobeying them. No matter how hard they tried, they couldn't keep all of God's rules all the time.

But God wasn't surprised. He knew they wouldn't be able to obey all the commandments, but He needed the people to realize this. You see, your mom and dad make rules to keep you safe, and so does God. But God knows that sometimes we mess up. So God made a way to save you and me when we sin. **All God wants from us is our hearts.** Back in Moses' time, God told the Israelites they could sacrifice an innocent, perfect-looking animal in their place. This had to be given in faith to pay for their sins. Salvation has always been by grace through faith. Why? Because God wanted His chosen people to know that sin leads to death, and they would always need forgiveness for their sins. There is always a price that has to be paid when we sin.

But one day, God's chosen people wouldn't have to sacrifice animals anymore to pay for their sins. This is because one day God was going to send Someone very special, Someone perfect, who could keep all the rules perfectly all the time. And that special Someone would lovingly die for everyone's sins once and for all. He was the greatest and final sacrifice.

Thank You, Lord, for taking care of Your people and for writing the Ten Commandments. Amen.

Prayer by Helena | FROM BRAZIL

Thoughts from Around the World

I know you have rules in your house. I do too. Maybe you can't eat candy every day, or riding your bike is only for after you finish your homework, or you have to go to bed early. I know that sometimes rules aren't fun, but they're made to protect us. We know that going to bed early isn't fun, but if you need to go to school in the morning, it's necessary to be well rested. Those who love us make these rules because they care for us. God gave Moses ten rules for His people to follow—to protect them and to keep them away from sin—because He loved them.

Don't feel bad if you get angry because you have to follow rules. Having rules shows you that you are loved. God is holy and wants us to walk in holiness, and following rules from our parents or teachers helps us learn to follow God's rules too.

Written by Giovanna | FROM BRAZIL

12

RAHAB AND THE BATTLE OF JERICHO

**NUMBERS 14;
DEUTERONOMY 31–34;
JOSHUA 2, 6**

Even after all the miracles God had performed for the Israelites, they still struggled—just like we do—to follow God's rules, to believe He loved them and wanted the best for them. So God led the Israelites through the wilderness for forty years as a punishment for their disobedience.

Eventually, God told Moses it was time for the Israelites to cross the Jordan River and head to the land He had promised them. He also told Moses, who was now 120 years old, that a new leader named Joshua would take the people into the Promised Land. But before Moses passed away, God brought him up to a high mountain so Moses could see the beautiful land that would soon belong to God's chosen people.

After Moses' death, Joshua began to lead the people. Joshua had been Moses' assistant, and as he spent years by Moses' side in the wilderness, Joshua saw how a great leader serves others.

As Joshua and the Israelites entered the Promised Land, they ran into a rather large problem—Jericho. Jericho was a *really* big city with *really* big walls to keep out people who wanted to enter the land. But inside this big city was a woman named Rahab.

Joshua sent two spies to Jericho so they could find out what the land was like. The spies secretly entered Jericho and ended up in Rahab's house. Soldiers of Jericho found out about the spies and went to Rahab's house to arrest them. But before the soldiers could get there, Rahab bravely hid the spies on her roof and covered them so they couldn't be seen. When the soldiers came to her house and asked about the spies, she told them they had already left her home and the city.

After the soldiers left, Rahab told the spies that she knew their God had given the Israelites the land they were entering. She had heard stories of how powerful the God of the Israelites was, and she knew their God was in control of everything in heaven and on earth. **Nothing was more powerful than the God of the Israelites.** So Rahab asked the spies to make an agreement with her. Since she bravely chose to hide them from the soldiers of Jericho, in return she asked the spies to protect her family when the Israelites came to take possession of the land. The spies agreed.

Rahab's house was built into the thick city wall of Jericho. Hanging a red rope out of her window, Rahab let the spies climb down and escape back to Joshua and their people. Later, when God brought down the walls of Jericho, the Israelites saw the red rope in Rahab's window and kept their promise. They protected Rahab and her family and allowed them to live with the Israelites.

Art by Simão | FROM PORTUGAL

Many years later, another Rescuer would come from Rahab's family and rescue the Israelites once again, but this time it would be Him hanging on a red-stained cross as He died for their sins.

God, help people who do not believe in You. Help them see You working in their lives. Please help people who don't know You to learn more about You. I want them to believe in You, like Rahab and her family did. Amen.

Prayer by Simão | FROM PORTUGAL

Thoughts from Around the World

Rahab was a Canaanite; she was not part of God's people. She didn't have a position of power. But she believed in God, and she wasn't afraid to risk her life for what was right. God saw her obedience and courage, and He saved her along with her family. Rahab's name is listed in the genealogy of Jesus.

I live in a city in Europe where believing in Jesus can be considered very strange. Rahab's story inspires me not to be afraid to do what is right in order to defend the name of my Savior. Like Rahab, I belong to the family of God because of Jesus. Do you also want to be a part of it, even if others around you find it strange?

Written by Ana | FROM PORTUGAL

13

DEBORAH

JUDGES 4–5

After many years, all the people in Joshua and Rahab's generation died, and a new generation was in charge. This generation didn't worship God and forgot His commandments. And because they didn't worship Him, they didn't love Him. And because they didn't love Him, they didn't obey Him. Instead of living their lives in obedience to God out of their love for Him, they decided to do what they thought was right in their own eyes. And the further they moved away from God, the worse life got for them. Whenever the Israelites would ignore God, different enemies would come and conquer them. Then the Israelites would feel sorry they had forgotten God and cry out for Him to save them.

In these days, the Israelites didn't have a king or queen ruling them. God alone was supposed to rule them. But when the Israelites cried out for God to rescue them, God would send a special person called a *judge* to help the Israelites follow Him again. Most of the time, these judges were warriors. They were selected by God to lead His people into battle against the enemies who had conquered them.

One of those judges was a woman named Deborah. Deborah was both wise and brave, and God used her to help His chosen people follow Him. At that time, the Israelites were being ruled by a powerful and evil king named Jabin who hated God's people. The Israelites were scared of him because his army was much bigger than theirs. But Deborah was not afraid. She knew God was with her and with the Israelites. She trusted God and knew they had nothing to fear when God was with them!

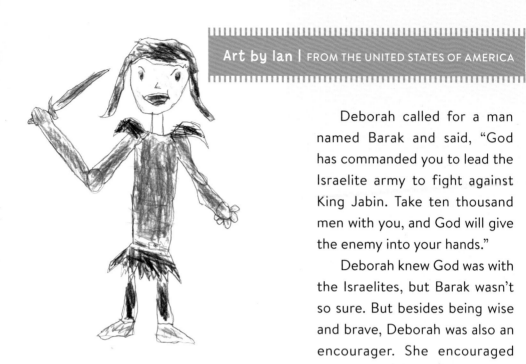

Deborah called for a man named Barak and said, "God has commanded you to lead the Israelite army to fight against King Jabin. Take ten thousand men with you, and God will give the enemy into your hands."

Deborah knew God was with the Israelites, but Barak wasn't so sure. But besides being wise and brave, Deborah was also an encourager. She encouraged Barak and reminded him that God was with him. Deborah even went into the battle with Barak. She was a warrior!

When the Israelites got to the battlefield, they met King Jabin's army, who was angry and ready to fight. But God was with the Israelites, just like He had promised. And the Israelites defeated King Jabin and his army.

After the battle and the Israelites' victory, Deborah showed her wisdom again: she led the people in praise and worship to God for the success He gave them. She sang a song of thankfulness to God, reminding her people that the victory came from God and God alone.

Like Deborah, we need to learn to be wise and brave as we face our battles, never forgetting that God is with us too. And when victories come our way, we also need to praise God and thank Him for the victory He has given us.

Dear God, I know that You are with me every day. Help me to be strong and wise and brave so I can do what is right. Amen.

Prayer by Ian | FROM THE UNITED STATES OF AMERICA

Thoughts from Around the World

In the Hausa language, the word for *war* is *yaki*. As a young girl I was faced with *yaki* like Deborah and the children of Israel. I lived in northern Nigeria then. That time was very painful, and I was frightened. The *yaki* I faced was because my family was being persecuted for being Christians. When my home was destroyed, my family and I became refugees. God surrounded us with good people who gave us food, clothing, and a place to stay. Their act of kindness encouraged me to be courageous, to keep on following God. Today I am telling people about the love of God and also translating Bible studies into Hausa. Just as God was with the children of Israel, He was with me and my family and provided help for us. Today I am still standing and telling others about God. He will fight for you during your battles too.

Written by Ebos | FROM NIGERIA

14

RUTH

During the time when judges like Deborah were leading Israel, there was a famine in the land. A woman named Naomi and her husband lived in the town of Bethlehem, and they didn't have enough to eat. So Naomi's husband decided to move his family to the nearby country of Moab. While in Moab, Naomi's two sons married two Moabite women, whose names were Orpah and Ruth.

While they were living in Moab, Naomi's husband and sons died, leaving Naomi and her two daughters-in-law as widows. Naomi was heartbroken. Soon after, Naomi heard the famine in Israel was over, so she decided to go back home. Since both of her daughters-in-law were still young women, Naomi encouraged them to find new husbands in Moab.

Art by Nadya | FROM UKRAINE

But neither daughter-in-law wanted to leave Naomi's side, for they both loved her so much. But Naomi encouraged them to stay. "Listen to me!" Naomi said. "Each of you should return to your mother's home. May the Lord bless you and help each of you to find a new husband."

Eventually, Orpah decided to stay in Moab, but Ruth still begged to go with Naomi. "Stop urging me to abandon you!" Ruth cried. **"Wherever you go, I will go too. And wherever you live, I will live there too. Your people will be my people. And the God you serve will be my God."**

So Naomi and Ruth headed to Bethlehem together. When they arrived, Naomi told her friends about the loss of her husband and sons in Moab. Because Ruth and Naomi were poor and needed food to eat, Ruth gathered grain in a nearby field. This was part of God's ultimate plan, for the field Ruth gathered grain in belonged to a kind and generous man named Boaz. And Boaz was related to Naomi's husband. In fact, Boaz's mother was Rahab, a woman who, years before, had also begun a new life among a new people.

Boaz had compassion for Ruth and Naomi when he learned their story. He allowed Ruth to gather as much grain as she needed so that she and Naomi would have more than enough food to eat. He even spoke to the other people working in his fields and asked them to be kind and treat Ruth well. Boaz marveled at Ruth's faithfulness to Naomi as she worked hard in his fields day after day.

Naomi was so happy that Ruth was working in Boaz's fields. She was grateful for his kindness as he went out of his way to make sure they had enough food to eat. Naomi hoped that one day Boaz and Ruth would get married. And they did! Together they had a son named Obed. Years later, Obed's grandson David would become the king of the Israelites. Boaz and Ruth's family was also the same family that Jesus came from, the One who redeemed the whole world!

Ruth showed unwavering faithfulness to Naomi, even in difficult circumstances. **But her faithfulness was rewarded!** God blessed Ruth with a new home, a new husband, and a new family. Naomi was blessed too, for she had a family to care for her and a grandson she could love and treasure.

God, help me trust You like Naomi and Ruth did. Please forgive our sins and make sure that all Ukrainians become believers and that I will have good dreams about unicorns. Amen.

Prayer by Nadya | FROM UKRAINE

Thoughts from Around the World

Imagine if you had to leave your home and move on your own to a strange town and school. You would have to meet new friends and teachers and find your new favorite meal in the cafeteria. That would feel so uncomfortable! The lives of Naomi and Ruth display the Lord's faithfulness and compassion in the hardest circumstances. Ruth didn't leave her mother-in-law alone when they had to move. And Boaz showed kindness to Ruth when she and Naomi had nothing to eat after returning to Israel. It is all a beautiful reflection of the Lord's steadfast love toward His people. There will be good and hard times in your life, but in all circumstances you can trust our God, who showed us the greatest love through sending Jesus. Thanks to Him, we are no longer strangers but beloved family members. And we will be sitting together at the feast next to our dearest Friend.

Written by Karina | FROM KAZAKHSTAN

15

HANNAH AND SAMUEL

1 SAMUEL 1–3

During the time of the judges, there was a woman named Hannah who wanted a baby more than anything else in the world. Hannah loved God very much, and she prayed to God every day, asking Him to bless her with a child of her own.

One day Hannah was especially sad because a woman who *did* have children was unkind to her. During the time Hannah lived, people treated women poorly if they couldn't have children. Hannah was so heartbroken that she went to the sanctuary to pray to God. She began to cry because she wanted a baby so badly. Hannah prayed, "O God, if You would look on the suffering of Your servant and give me a baby boy, then I promise I will dedicate him to You all the days of his life."

While she was praying, Hannah cried so much that she no longer had words to pray, only tears. A priest at the sanctuary named Eli saw her tears and approached her. Hannah explained to Eli that she was pouring out her heart to God. Eli replied, "May God give you what you have asked for." Hannah then left the sanctuary and was no longer sad.

Soon after this, God answered Hannah's prayers. Hannah became pregnant with a baby boy. She named him Samuel, which means "I asked the Lord for him." Hannah was so thankful to God for answering her prayer this way that she dedicated the child to God, just like she said she would. She wanted this baby boy to serve God all the days of his life and to love God as much as she did.

And that's exactly what happened. When Samuel was no longer a baby, Hannah remembered her promise to God and brought him to the sanctuary and to Eli the priest so that Samuel could learn to serve God. And that's what Samuel did.

One night, when Samuel was a young boy, God called him by name. Samuel heard God's voice, but he thought it was Eli calling for him, so he ran into Eli's room to see what he needed. But Eli hadn't called him. Three times the boy heard his name, and three times the boy ran to Eli. Finally, a very tired Eli realized what was happening. He told Samuel, "Go back and lie down. When God calls you again, say, 'Speak, Lord. Your servant is listening.'" So Samuel went back to bed and did what Eli told him to do.

Art by Isabel | FROM COLOMBIA

When God spoke again, Samuel answered. God then told the boy what he needed to know about the future of God's people, for Samuel would grow up to become an important prophet. For the rest of his life, Samuel listened to God and told God's people what He wanted them to know.

Both Hannah and Samuel had hearts that wanted to know God and serve Him. God spoke to them in His timing and His way. Hannah and Samuel trusted God and obeyed Him, knowing that God always has a plan for our lives.

Lord, thank You for always answering our prayers. Although sometimes You do not answer them as we would like, You always give us what we need. Help me to hear and obey Your voice. Amen.

Prayer by Isabel | FROM COLOMBIA

Thoughts from Around the World

In the story of Hannah and Samuel, we learn two important things. First, God hears us. Hannah longed with all her heart to have a child. She prayed to God, and God heard her. God says that whatever we ask of Him according to His will, He will grant to us. So, if there is something you are looking forward to today, go and tell God. He will listen to you. Second, we must learn to listen to God. Samuel lived in the sanctuary and was learning all about God. When he understood that God was speaking to him, he listened attentively and obeyed. God now speaks to us through the Bible. And when reading the Bible, you must pay close attention to understand what God is saying to you and wants you to do. Then you will always have a heart that trusts and obeys God.

Written by Zulay | FROM COLOMBIA

16

DAVID AND GOLIATH

1 SAMUEL 17

When Samuel was a prophet for Israel, there lived a shepherd boy named David. David was young, but he was incredibly brave. What was most important about David, though, was that he loved God with all his heart. His love for God made him courageous and full of faith.

David was the youngest of eight brothers. While his three oldest brothers were fighting against Israel's enemy, the Philistines, David was in the fields taking care of his father's sheep. One day David's father asked him to bring some food to his brothers and check on them.

While David was at the battlefield, he heard a Philistine who stood over nine feet tall challenge the Israelites. The giant's name was Goliath, and Goliath wanted the Israelites to send their best warrior to fight him. Whoever won that fight would rule over the group of people who lost. The Israelites didn't have a warrior as big and tall as Goliath. They were all afraid of him. But David wasn't.

You see, God had been working in David's life, making him strong and brave long before David ever came face-to-face with this giant of a man. Out in the fields, David had already learned how to kill a lion and a bear to keep his father's sheep safe. God had protected David then, and he knew that God would protect him again.

When none of the men in the Israelite army wanted to fight the giant Goliath, young David volunteered. David went to the king of Israel, whose name was Saul. At first, King Saul thought it was a joke. How could this young boy fight a giant like Goliath? But David was brave and insisted that God was with him, and he could indeed fight Goliath and win.

King Saul said to David, "You can't fight this giant. You're a child! Goliath is an experienced fighter. He has been in the Philistine army since he was young."

Finally King Saul agreed to let David fight, but he wanted David to wear his special armor for protection. But the armor was too big and heavy for David. Instead, David decided to use a tool he knew how to use. He picked up five smooth stones and his sling and went out to fight the giant.

When Goliath saw David approach him, he mocked David, laughing that the Israelites would send a boy to fight a man's battle. But David stood firm in his faith in God and said, **"You come to me with a sword and with a spear and with a javelin, but I come to you in the name of the God of Israel!"** Then with one swift move, David used his sling to fling a stone right into Goliath's forehead, causing him to fall to the ground and die.

David defeated Goliath because his faith in God was more powerful than his fear. David proved that how we look on the outside isn't important—but who we get our power and courage from *is*.

Art by Nehemiah | FROM THAILAND

David's victory over Goliath amazed everyone, and it showed that even the smallest and seemingly weakest person could overcome their fears when they placed their faith in God. David showed that true power comes not from physical strength but from faith in God.

Lord, help us to rely on Your strength to defeat the giants in our lives. Amen.

Prayer by Nehemiah | FROM THAILAND

Thoughts from Around the World

Do you have a giant in your life? Sometimes we have things in front of us that seem impossible or scary. David looked straight at Goliath, and he wasn't scared at all. He didn't even think it was impossible for him to win! No one was cheering for David when he went to fight Goliath. They thought it was impossible. But David trusted in the Lord, and he knew with God all things were possible. He was shocked that everyone was letting Goliath mock God. David didn't fight Goliath alone. He had God on his side, and he knew God would win this battle. Always remember you are never alone. God is always with you. Trust in Him like David did, and don't fear the giants in your life. In faith, face them with God by your side.

Written by Vicky | FROM THE UNITED STATES OF AMERICA AND THAILAND

17

DAVID AND JONATHAN

1 SAMUEL 18–20; 2 SAMUEL 1–2

After David killed Goliath, King Saul wanted David to work for him. When David started working for King Saul, he became best friends with King Saul's son Jonathan. **Both David and Jonathan loved God very much.** And their friendship was so close that they promised that no matter what, they would always look out for each other and their families.

Over time, King Saul became jealous of David. Whenever David was praised by the Israelites for being strong and courageous in battle, King Saul got angry because *he* wanted that praise and applause. He didn't want the people to like David more than they liked him. King Saul even wanted the praise of the people *more* than he wanted to please God. So King Saul plotted to kill David. This shows how dangerous jealousy can be. It can make you want to hurt people who are doing nothing wrong.

Art by Ellie | FROM TAIWAN

When Jonathan found out that his father wanted David dead, he was very upset. But Jonathan was a good friend, and just because his father didn't like David didn't mean Jonathan couldn't. One day when King Saul was planning to hurt David, Jonathan found out about the plan and warned David that he needed to run away and hide until King Saul was no longer angry at him.

David was able to escape King Saul's evil plan because of Jonathan's help, but David couldn't return home for a long time. David and Jonathan were really sad that they wouldn't be able to see each other as much as they used to. But they remembered that no matter what, they would always and forever look after each other and their families.

A little while later King Saul and Jonathan were in a fierce battle fighting one of Israel's enemies, and they both died. When David heard the news, he was heart-broken. His loyal and trustworthy best friend was gone, and he missed him dearly.

After King Saul died, David became king. But he remembered his promise to his best friend, Jonathan, and he made sure to look after Jonathan's family.

David and Jonathan's friendship was a beautiful example of loyalty, kindness, and love. Their bond was unbreakable, even when it was challenged by jealousy and danger. They showed that true friendship can stand the test of time and can be a source of strength and joy.

Dear God, it is easy to feel jealous. Please take jealousy away and help us. In Jesus' name, amen.

Prayer by Ellie | FROM TAIWAN

Thoughts from Around the World

In China where I come from, disobeying a parent is never encouraged, let alone saying no to the king. Can you imagine a young person questioning and challenging people who are older and in a higher position than they are? The relationships between a king and his people and parents and their children were the most foundational human relationships in ancient China, like they were in Israel. Yet Jonathan turned them all upside down, because he loved his Lord and had sworn to do what was right in the sight of God by protecting his friend. Jonathan displayed loyal friendship when he put David's life higher than his own. He kept his word to his friend and honored God. When what the world asks of you is different from what is right in the sight of God, it's comforting to know that God will honor loyal friendship that honors Him.

Written by Vivian | FROM CHINA

18

ELISHA AND THE WIDOW

2 KINGS 4:1–7

In the land of Israel many years after the time of King David, there lived a poor widow and her two sons. One day a creditor came to the widow's house and told her she had to pay all the money she owed him. He threatened that if she didn't, he would take her two sons and make them his servants. Understandably, the widow was very upset. She didn't know what to do to save her boys. Then she remembered the prophet Elisha lived nearby, so she went to see him for advice.

"Elisha, you know my husband is dead, and I am very poor. A creditor came to my house today and said if I didn't pay the debt I owed him, he would take away my two boys and make them his servants. I'm so upset! I have nothing but a small jar of olive oil. What should I do?"

Elisha replied, "Go and ask all your friends for as many empty jars as they have. Get as many as you can. Then go home, close the door behind you, and begin pouring the olive oil into the jars."

Art by Elija | FROM LITHUANIA

The widow did exactly as she was told. She and her sons gathered a lot of empty jars, closed the door, and began to fill them. **First, one empty jar was filled, then another, and another.** As soon as all the jars were filled to the top, the olive oil from her small jar stopped flowing.

The widow was so excited that she immediately went back to Elisha and told him the good news.

Elisha said, "Now go and sell all the olive oil you have. You can pay the creditor what you owe him, and then you and your sons can live off the rest of the profit!"

God had answered the cries of the widow's heart, for God took what little she had and multiplied it to meet her needs. Now she didn't have to look to the future with worry. God had provided for her!

Dear God, I trust that only You can take care of me. Please be in my heart every day and talk to me. Amen.

Prayer by Elija | FROM LITHUANIA

Thoughts from Around the World

We as human beings want to protect and take care of ourselves. We use anything and everything we have to make sure we survive. But we have our limits. God knows it. He wants to take care of us because He has no limits. He doesn't force us to trust Him but gives us a choice. Our heavenly Father waits until we start trusting in Him and His plan, not ourselves. When we stop thinking the things we have can save and protect us, God steps in. He takes what little we have and multiples it. He appreciates when we give to Him everything we have and trust Him to provide us what we actually need (1 Kings 17:8–16; Mark 12:41–44; John 6:8–11).

Written by Morta | FROM LITHUANIA

19

JONAH

JONAH 1–4

I n the land of Israel there was a man named Jonah. Like Samuel, Jonah was a prophet, which meant that he would tell the people truths about God, and God would tell Jonah what He wanted him to do.

But one day, to Jonah's surprise, God said He wanted Jonah to go to the city of Nineveh and tell the people there about Him. Now, it's important to understand that Jonah did *not* like the people living in Nineveh. They were wicked people, and their country was one of Israel's worst enemies. So Jonah didn't want to go to Nineveh. He didn't believe they deserved God's forgiveness or love.

Instead of obeying God and walking east toward Nineveh, Jonah got in a boat and sailed west—the exact *opposite* direction from Nineveh! As Jonah sat in the boat, a wind began to stir. At first, it was just a few dark clouds, a soft breeze, and light raindrops. But before long, the ship was in the middle of a fierce storm. The storm got so bad that even the sailors were scared and didn't know what to do.

"We're sinking! Throw all the cargo overboard!" they cried out, and they tossed their cargo into the sea.

"You must throw me overboard," Jonah told the sailors.

The sailors knew Jonah had been running from God. But they didn't want to throw him overboard. The men tried to row back to land, but the storm just kept growing worse.

"Throw me in," Jonah said. "And the seas will calm down for you."

And, with heavy hearts, they did. As soon as Jonah hit the water, the storm stopped! The sailors were amazed.

Jonah thought for sure this was the end for him. He had run from what God wanted him to do, and look where it had gotten him: sinking in the sea! But the moment the storm started, God set Jonah's rescue plan on its way. A big fish was headed toward Jonah to swallow him whole and save him from drowning. Before Jonah realized what happened to him, there was sudden darkness. At first, he thought maybe he had died, but then he felt the slimy insides of the fish and realized he had not.

Poor Jonah was scared and didn't know what to do. **So he began to pray and talk to God.** For three whole days, Jonah sat in the belly of that giant fish, thinking and praying. Jonah was wrong not to obey God and tell the people of Nineveh about Him. It is never right to hate a group of people, because we are all made in God's image and worthy in His sight.

As Jonah sat in the dark, slimy belly of the giant fish, he had plenty of time to think about his actions. He realized he had been wrong to disobey God and run away from what God had asked him to do.

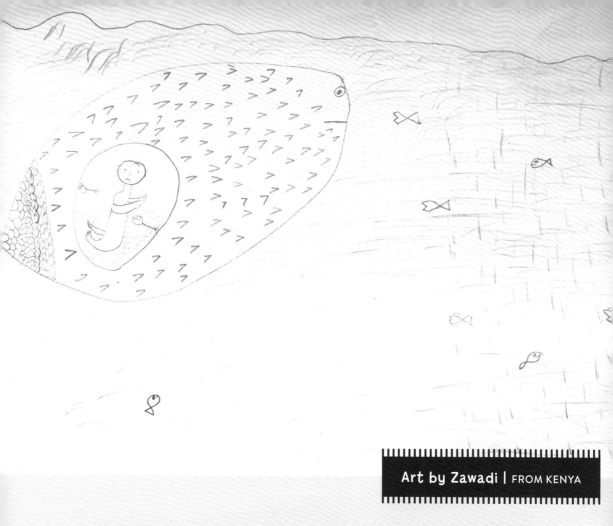

In that moment, Jonah understood how good and kind God is. God wanted the people of Nineveh to know about Him and have an opportunity to repent for the evil things they had done. But because Jonah disliked them so much, Jonah had tried to take that opportunity away from them. And that was wrong of him.

So Jonah hoped God would give him another chance. If He would, then Jonah would obey God this time and go to Nineveh, just as he had been asked. And you know what? God heard Jonah's prayers, even inside the belly of that giant fish in the deep ocean waters. For no matter how far away we try to run from God, we are never so far away that God can't hear our prayers.

After three days, God had the fish spit Jonah onto the shore. Jonah, though a little stinky, was so relieved to be alive! After Jonah was back on dry land, God once again asked him to go to Nineveh. This time, Jonah obeyed immediately. He told the people of Nineveh about God and how they needed to stop doing wicked things or their town would be punished for all the evil things they had done.

And you know what? They listened! Much to Jonah's surprise, the people of Nineveh heard his message and believed! All the people, including the king of the city, repented from their wicked ways, hoping God would help them and show them mercy. And God did just that! He spared the city, because the people of Nineveh were truly sorry and asked for forgiveness.

Both Jonah and the people of Nineveh disobeyed God. But in God's unending mercy, He gave them both a second chance. And great news: He does the same for us too!

God, I thank You for protecting us and forgiving us. May You give us courage to do whatever You want us to do. Amen.

Prayer by Zawadi | FROM KENYA

Thoughts from Around the World

Jonah was a prophet chosen by God to deliver an important message to the people of Nineveh. But Jonah was scared because the people of Nineveh were his enemies and had done many bad things. He tried to run away from God's command and ended up in a big storm. To save the others on his ship, Jonah told them to throw him overboard. As soon as he hit the water, the storm stopped. God sent a big fish to swallow Jonah, where he spent three days praying and realizing his mistake. When the fish spit him out, Jonah obeyed God and went to Nineveh. The people listened to his message and changed their ways. Jonah learned that even when things are scary, it's important to do the right thing.

Written by Stella | FROM KENYA

20

SHADRACH, MESHACH, AND ABEDNEGO

As time passed, God's people stopped trusting Him and began disobeying Him again. Finally, because of their stubborn disobedience, the Israelites were conquered by the Babylonians. The Babylonians took many of the Israelites and sent them as exiles to Babylon, a place far from their homes in the Promised Land.

Now the king of Babylon was very powerful, and everything he told his people to do, they did. So when the king had a giant golden statue made for his people to worship, everyone bowed down to worship it—except for three brave young men named Shadrach, Meshach, and Abednego. **When everyone else bowed, these Israelites refused and stood tall.** They loved God and knew that bowing down to an idol was wrong, no matter how big or shiny it was.

When the king saw these young men refuse to bow down to his idol, he became furious. He was so furious that he wanted to make an example out of them so that no one else would dare to disobey his orders. The king told his soldiers to turn up the heat in his royal fiery furnace, tie up the three young men, and throw them into the fire! He wanted to show his people what happens to those who disobey the king's orders.

95

To the king's surprise, when he looked inside the blazing furnace, he saw *four* men, not three! How could this be? Just as surprising, not one of the men was being burned in the fire! As the king looked closer, he realized the fourth man with Shadrach, Meshach, and Abednego was an angel. Immediately the king ordered the men to come out of the blazing furnace, for he couldn't believe his eyes. When Shadrach, Meshach, and Abednego walked out of the furnace, they weren't burned at all. In fact, they didn't even smell like smoke. This was impossible!

At that moment, the king realized he was wrong. The God these three young men loved and worshiped was the one true God. It was wrong for him to make these young men worship his man-made god. The king then told his people they should not speak against the one true God who protected these three brave and loyal young men. **The God who would go into the fire with these young men and protect them is the one true God.**

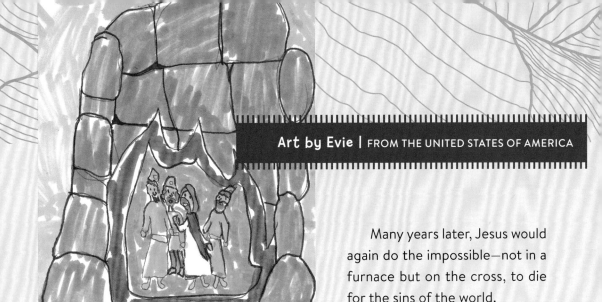

Many years later, Jesus would again do the impossible—not in a furnace but on the cross, to die for the sins of the world.

Dear God, please help me to stand up for what is right, no matter what other people say. Help me to be strong. Be with me, no matter where I am. Amen.

Prayer by Evie | FROM THE UNITED STATES OF AMERICA

Thoughts from Around the World

It must have been so hard for these three young men to stand up for what was right! I lived in Singapore when I was younger. There are temples there that not only house statues of false gods but also host shrines of our ancestors. I was forced to take up incense sticks and worship both! When I refused to obey, my elders thought I was disrespectful and ungrateful to my ancestors. Family is everything to a little Chinese girl, and I felt so torn! But I knew there is no other god other than the one true God, and I should not be bowing down to any other gods.

Written by Yating | FROM SINGAPORE

21

DANIEL IN THE LIONS' DEN

DANIEL 6

Like Shadrach, Meshach, and Abednego, Daniel was also a Jewish exile living in Babylon. One day, an empire called Persia conquered Babylon, and a new king named Darius was put in charge. Daniel worked as an advisor to King Darius, which meant the Persian king thought Daniel was smart and gave great advice. But the most important thing about Daniel was that he loved God with all his heart. Every day, Daniel would wake up early in the morning and pray to God. He would pray three times every day! Daniel loved talking to God!

But not all the king's advisors liked Daniel. Some were jealous of him because King Darius thought Daniel was the smartest of them all. So they got together to figure out how to get Daniel in trouble. The other advisors watched Daniel every day, but to their surprise they never saw him doing anything wrong. Then one of the sneaky advisors noticed Daniel went to his room every day to pray. So these jealous advisors devised a plan. They'd trick the king into making a law that said no one could pray to anyone or anything except the king—or they'd be thrown into a den of lions!

When the king passed the law, Daniel had a choice to make: obey God or obey the king's new law. Daniel knew what the right answer was. He would continue to pray to God, even if it meant breaking the law and risking his life. Obeying God is always the right answer. So, as usual, three times a day Daniel would go to his room, where his windows opened up toward the city, and pray to God. Of course, it didn't take long for the jealous advisors to catch poor Daniel praying, and they happily ran to tell King Darius.

"Oh, marvelous and wonderful King, doesn't your new law say that everyone has to pray to you and only you?"

"Yes," said King Darius. "Why?"

"Well, most magnificent King, we just saw Daniel praying to his God and not obeying your new law."

When the jealous advisors reported this, King Darius was sad because he liked Daniel. He knew he had been tricked, but there was nothing he could do. He had to enforce the law.

So with tears in his eyes and worry in his heart, the king ordered Daniel to be thrown into the lions' den. Poor Daniel! He was scared, but he also knew God was with him. As soldiers put Daniel in the lions' den, the king called out, "Daniel, I hope the God that you love so much rescues you!"

That night the king couldn't sleep. He tossed and turned in bed, worrying about Daniel and what could be happening to him. The king felt terrible about the new law he had been tricked into making. As soon as the first rays of sunlight showed in the morning sky, the king jumped out of bed and ran to see how Daniel was.

"Daniel, Daniel, are you okay? Has your God saved you?" the king cried out, fearing the worst.

"Yes!" brave Daniel replied. "My God sent a mighty angel to close the mouths of the lions. I am not hurt at all!"

The king was amazed. And at that moment, he realized Daniel's God was the one true God, and he praised Him for rescuing Daniel. Then the king made another new law that said Daniel's God was the one true God, and everyone needed to worship Daniel's God instead.

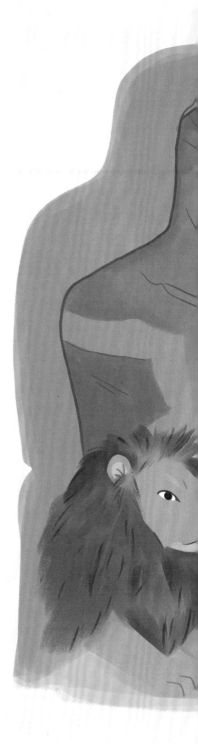

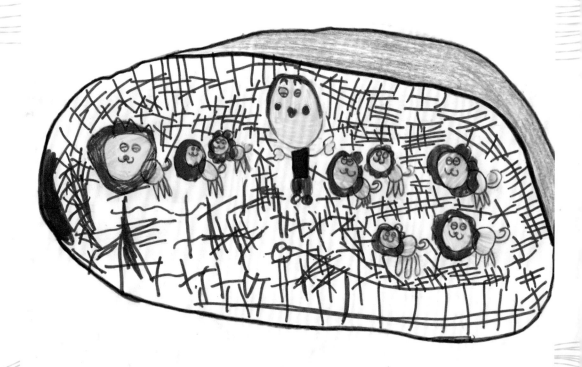

Daniel was so thankful that God protected him in the lions' den. He knew he could always count on God to help him in times of trouble. So Daniel continued to pray to God every day, thanking Him for His love and protection. And he never forgot how much God loved him and how He had rescued him.

Lord, thank You for always taking care of me, just like You took care of Daniel. And thank You for taking care of my family too. Amen.

Prayer by Lizz | FROM COLOMBIA

Thoughts from Around the World

In my country of Colombia, there is an area called the Eastern Plains, which is full of extensive savannas. The houses are very far apart, so you have to walk up to an hour to get from one house to another. One day when my husband was a child, he had to go to the neighbor's house. When he had already walked a long way, he saw that a huge tiger was walking toward him, and he got very scared! He ran and got behind a tree and started praying! Suddenly the tiger went in another direction. God heard his prayer!

You and I may never have to face a ferocious animal like Daniel and my husband did, but we do go through moments that make us feel afraid. Like Daniel, you can pray and be assured that God will help you. He loves you and is always with you.

Written by Zulay | FROM COLOMBIA

22

ESTHER

After the time of Daniel, in the land of Persia, there lived a king named Xerxes. King Xerxes was very rich and powerful. He had everything he ever wanted, including a beautiful wife named Queen Vashti.

One night King Xerxes was having a fancy party for all his officials and servants at the palace, and he invited Queen Vashti to attend. At the party, King Xerxes wanted to show off his beautiful queen to all his guests. But Queen Vashti didn't think that was a great idea and refused to go.

The queen's refusal made the king's face turn red because she embarrassed him in front of all his friends. King Xerxes got very angry and told her she could no longer be queen.

Before long, King Xerxes' officials went out and began looking for the most beautiful women in the kingdom. They would find the new queen by holding a sort of beauty contest. All the most beautiful women in Persia who weren't married had to enter the contest. The contest winner didn't get money or a fancy sash to wear around; the winner would marry the king and become the next queen of Persia!

At this time, a beautiful young Jewish woman named Esther lived in Persia. Now Esther was more than just beautiful; she was also wise, obedient, and courageous. Growing up, Esther did not have an easy life. She was an orphan raised by her cousin, Mordecai. **Esther was many things, but the most important thing about Esther was that she loved God.**

When the beauty contest began, King Xerxes picked Esther out of all the beautiful women in Persia as his next queen. Of course, the king may have selected Esther because of her beauty, but God knew that her beauty went far beyond what people could see. For Esther not only had a beautiful face but also a brave and beautiful heart.

Now one of King Xerxes' officials was an evil man named Haman. Haman hated Jewish people, especially Esther's cousin Mordecai. Haman hated Mordecai because Mordecai wouldn't bow down to him.

Mordecai only bowed down to honor God. Because of his hatred for Mordecai and the Jewish people, Haman devised an evil plan to kill them all. Haman used his influence to get King Xerxes to sign a law that said *all* the Jews living in Persia would all be killed on a certain day.

When Mordecai heard the news about the law, he shared the news with Esther immediately. He saw God's hand of protection on the Jewish people because the king had chosen Esther, a Jew, as his queen. When Esther had first gone to the palace, Mordecai had told Esther not to tell anyone she was a Jew, because he knew people like Haman might have put Esther in danger. But now Mordecai saw that Esther had a chance to save her people. "You have been made queen for such a time as this," Mordecai told Esther. "God has placed you in this position to help save our people."

Esther knew she needed to go to King Xerxes and try to stop this evil plan, but she was very scared. It was against the law to visit the king without being invited. But God was giving Esther the opportunity to save her people from Haman's evil plan. So, even though she was afraid, Esther knew she could be brave because God was with her. God's invisible hands were all over Esther's story. **Just because we don't see God doesn't mean He isn't working and orchestrating events to protect His people.** Nothing is a coincidence with God.

So Esther prayed and fasted for three days. She asked her friends and the rest of the Jewish community to pray and fast with her too. Then she approached King Xerxes, not knowing what his response would be. Esther placed her life in God's hands and walked forward in obedience.

When Esther approached the king, he was happy to see her. He asked what she wanted, and she said, "If it pleases the king, I would like you and Haman to come to a banquet that I will prepare for you." The king agreed, and Haman was excited to be invited to such a special banquet with the queen. Haman even bragged about being invited to the queen's banquet to his family and friends.

Haman thought he was being honored by being invited to this special dinner. But during the meal, Esther revealed that she was a Jew and that Haman had tricked the king into signing a decree to kill all the Jews in the kingdom, including her. The king was furious that someone would plot against his queen and her people, and he had Haman killed immediately. On the terrible day the Jews were supposed to be killed, King Xerxes gave them permission to defend themselves, and Haman's plan was defeated.

God was with Esther. She had become queen of Persia at just the right time to save her people from destruction. Esther was brave and obedient because she knew God was with her every step of the way *for such a time as this.*

Jesus, if someone tries to hurt my sister, I stand in front of her, because she is little. If someone tries to hurt me, may You stand in front of me to defend me. Amen.

Prayer by Júlia | FROM BRAZIL

Thoughts from Around the World

Esther was just a young woman. She was an orphan, and her people served the king of Persia. It might have been scary to be carried to the king's palace, alone, to be married to him and made queen. When I was young, my family moved to another country. Everything was different, including the language and the food. I had to go to a new school and learn many things about a different people. I missed my friends, and sometimes I was very lonely, so I understand how Esther felt. But she was obedient, and God worked with her and through her to save her people. It was not by her strength, wisdom, or power but by God's strength, wisdom, and power that the Jews were saved. It doesn't matter who we are but who our God is. If we are obedient and trust Him, He will use us to bless and save others!

Written by Phoenix Maria | FROM BRAZIL

BETWEEN THE OLD AND NEW TESTAMENT

Between the Old Testament and the New Testament, there is a gap of time—about four hundred years—when no biblical books were written. Sometimes, people have said that God must have been silent during this time. That would be a super long time for God to be silent, wouldn't it?

But was God really silent? Even when we are quiet, we can still show love, can't we? A hug, a smile, or even just sitting close by can speak volumes. God was like that during this time. Even though God did not speak through His prophets during this time and none of our biblical books talk about this period of time, God was still at work in those years, preparing the most amazing thing the world had ever seen: the arrival of Jesus!

During this time, God was like a gardener, carefully preparing the soil for beautiful plants to spring up and grow. He was getting everything ready so that when Jesus came, the hearts of His children would be ready to receive Him and understand His love.

We should remember that even when God seems quiet, He is always with us, working in ways we might not see or understand right away. This period between the Old Testament and the New Testament reminds us that even when we can't see God moving or hear His voice, we can trust that He is still working on our behalf and that good things are on the way.

So, as you turn these pages and continue reading through God's grand story, remember that even though we have no biblical books that describe these years, God was still preparing the world for the greatest gift of all—Jesus! And in your own moments of silence, when it seems God isn't speaking, remember that He is always with you.

For even when God might seem to be silent, He is still working behind the scenes.

NEW TESTAMENT

23

ANNOUNCEMENT OF JESUS' BIRTH

LUKE 1

After so many years of rescuing His people, God was about to put His greatest rescue mission in place. Throughout the Old Testament, God was foreshadowing the arrival of the Promised One who would finally, once and for all, rescue every person. This Promised One would fulfill all the prophecies made about Him from the beginning of time. He would bring heaven to earth.

In His magnificent wisdom, God chose to use a young woman to help bring God Himself into the world as a little baby. This young woman's name was Mary.

Mary lived in a small town called Nazareth in Israel. She was engaged to a man named Joseph. Both Mary and Joseph loved God very much.

One day, an angel named Gabriel suddenly appeared to Mary. At first, she was startled and scared. She had never seen an angel before! *What does he want with me?* she wondered.

"Do not be afraid, Mary," the angel Gabriel said to her kindly. "I have good news to tell you. God is with you, Mary! God has chosen you of all the young women in the world."

Mary couldn't believe what she was hearing! *Why me?* she thought.

"Mary, God has chosen you to be the mother of His Son. You will name Him Jesus. People will call Jesus 'great' and 'Son of the Most High.' God will give Jesus the throne of His ancestor King David, and on that throne Jesus will reign forever. His kingdom will never end," Gabriel said.

That was a lot of information for Mary to take in all at once.

"But how can this be?" asked Mary as she tried to understand.

"Mary," the angel Gabriel said lovingly, "God is all-powerful. He can do anything. Nothing is impossible for God."

So even though Mary didn't understand how she would become a mother, she trusted God. She knew God loved her and everything He did was good.

"I am God's servant," Mary said, "and I will serve Him all the days of my life. I trust God. My life is His, and I will obey Him."

Thank You, Jesus, for coming down to earth to be with us and for dying for us. You are bigger and greater than any of us, and so much more powerful too. Thank You, God. Amen.

Prayer by Anita | FROM ITALY

Thoughts from Around the World

In Italy where I live, there are a lot of statues and paintings of Mary because she is very important to the Christians living here. She often looks like an adult woman with a sad expression. But Christian historians believe Mary was young when the angel visited her. And though she was afraid of the angel, Mary reacted to his news with joy and obeyed God. She even sang a beautiful song for the occasion (Luke 1:46–55). She was given a difficult task: to be the mother of Jesus Himself! Yet she trusted that God would help her because He had already helped so many people over so many years. Truly, Mary was a blessed girl! Every time I see a statue or painting of Mary in my country, I always think about this young girl's faithfulness and how God called Mary for such an important task.

Written by Gloria | FROM ITALY

24

JESUS' BIRTH

LUKE 2:1–21

Nine months after the angel visited, Mary was ready to give birth to baby Jesus any day. But then, the Roman emperor, who ruled over all the land in Israel, ordered a census where everyone in the land needed to be counted. So Joseph and a very pregnant Mary had to go on a long journey from Nazareth to Bethlehem, the town of King David, where Joseph was born.

When they arrived at Bethlehem, Mary was tired from traveling for so long. Her body hurt all over, and she needed to rest. But to Mary and Joseph's disappointment, there wasn't any place for them to stay in Bethlehem. The whole town was filled with people waiting to be counted. Every room was full; every bed was taken.

Art by Brinnley | FROM THE UNITED STATES OF AMERICA

But Joseph kept trying to find somewhere to stay. Surely there was someplace he and Mary could rest. From looking at Mary, Joseph knew baby Jesus would be arriving soon.

Finally, just when Joseph and Mary were about to give up, one innkeeper said, "I don't have a room or bed for you in my inn. But I do have a stable where I keep my animals. You are welcome to stay there."

Of all the most beautiful, majestic places for God to enter into the world in human form, He chose a stinky stable with stinky animals. The King of all kings would come into the world in a way that no one expected.

There in that stinky stable, the promised Rescuer arrived. Mary gave birth to Jesus in the glory of the ordinary. God's greatest gift had finally arrived.

With her heart full of wonder and love, Mary wrapped baby Jesus in swaddling clothes to keep Him warm. She placed God's Son in a manger, where the stinky stable animals ate their food.

A small distance away from the town, shepherds were caring for their sheep on the rolling hills. Suddenly a bright light pierced the night sky and took the shepherds by surprise. A mighty angel appeared out of the darkness and stood before the ordinary shepherds. Like Mary, the shepherds were shocked and surprised by what they saw, and they quickly became afraid.

"Don't be afraid," the angel told them. "I have come to tell you some news—good news for the whole world that will change your lives and the lives of those who come after you. The promised Rescuer has finally arrived! God's Son, Christ the Lord, has been born in the town of David, just as was promised! Go and see Him. You will find your long-awaited Redeemer, God's gift to the world, lying in a manger and wrapped in swaddling clothes."

Suddenly the inky-black sky filled with an army of angels, all praising God and singing, "Glory to God in the highest, and on earth peace to all people for all time!" Then, just as quickly as the angels appeared, they disappeared.

The shepherds stood there, amazed at all they had just experienced. They couldn't believe it, and joy filled their hearts. "Let's go see this Promised Child, our long-awaited Rescuer," they said to each other. So the shepherds immediately left in search of baby Jesus. And like all who search for Him, the shepherds found Him. Jesus was lying in a manger, just as the angel had described.

When they found Mary and Joseph with baby Jesus, the shepherds told them about what they had experienced and what the angel had said about Jesus. Mary listened closely to what the shepherds shared and held their testimonies close to her heart.

After the shepherds left baby Jesus, they couldn't stop talking about Him and glorifying God for this amazing news. Their long-awaited Rescuer had finally arrived, a baby who the prophet Isaiah called *Immanuel*, which means "God with us" (Isaiah 7:14). **Their Savior had been born!**

Jesus, thank You for coming down to earth as a baby. You are the best present of all. Nothing compares to You. You are amazing! I am so thankful for You! Amen.

Prayer by Brinnley | FROM THE UNITED STATES OF AMERICA

Thoughts from Around the World

For thousands of years, in many different cultures, rulers asked to count their people in something called a "census." This also happened in China, where I am from, at least three hundred years before Christ. Until modern times, traveling to be counted in a census wasn't very easy, but it's something people had to do. Of course Mary and Joseph found this to be true. And even though they couldn't stay in an inn with a bed, they were able to stay in a stable, where they were visited by shepherds, proclaiming the words of an angel and praising God for His merciful rescuing work. Mary and Joseph were remembered by God, and they were cared for by God, the heavenly Ruler. God, our true Ruler and King, cares for us. And He uses the circumstances and people around us to fulfill His will. May we treasure His works in our hearts and one day join the heavenly chorus singing, "Glory to God in the highest, and on earth peace among those with whom he is pleased!" (Luke 2:14 ESV).

Written by Vivian | FROM CHINA

25

JESUS IN THE TEMPLE

LUKE 2:41–52

Twelve years had passed since Jesus' birth. One day, Jesus traveled with His parents and many other families from where they lived to Jerusalem to celebrate the special holiday of Passover, when the Jewish people remembered how God rescued them from the Egyptians. Remembering God's faithfulness and how He has helped us through the years is always important.

After celebrating Passover with their family and friends, Mary and Joseph started their journey back home with their group. Mary and Joseph thought Jesus was with them, but they were wrong! Jesus wasn't anywhere to be found.

Mary and Joseph were shocked and felt terrible! How could they have let this happen? Frantically they went from friend to friend and relative to relative, asking if they had seen Jesus. They all answered the same: the last time they saw Jesus was back in Jerusalem!

So quickly, Mary and Joseph turned around and headed back to Jerusalem, searching for Jesus. For three days they looked everywhere and asked everyone they met if they had seen Jesus. Finally, on the third day, they decided to go to the temple

courts. To their surprise, they found Jesus sitting among the religious teachers, who were listening to Him and asking Him questions. These teachers were amazed at Jesus' wisdom at such a young age and His deep understanding of Scripture. **But they didn't realize who they were talking to: God in the flesh.**

Mary, her heart relieved when she saw her son, rushed over to Jesus. "Why didn't You go back home with us? Your father and I have been looking for You for days. We've been so worried and scared, searching for You night and day!"

Jesus replied, "Why were you searching for Me? I've been here all along in My Father's house, just as I should be."

Mary and Joseph didn't understand what Jesus meant, but they took Him back home all the same. So Jesus returned to Nazareth, obeying His earthly parents like He obeyed His heavenly Father.

As Jesus grew from a young boy to a man, His wisdom grew. And as Mary watched with amazement as her son grew up, she treasured all these things in her heart. Her wonderful boy grew into a strong and wise man, someone people loved and admired—and God did too. Soon the day would come when people would begin to see God's wise rescue plan begin to unfold.

Jesus, please help me to obey God all the days of my life. And help me to listen to my mommy and daddy as they teach me about You. Amen.

Prayer by Jonas | FROM POLAND AND CANADA

Thoughts from Around the World

Have you ever gotten lost when you were out with your parents? It can be really scary! I can only imagine how Mary and Joseph felt as they frantically searched for Jesus for three days. But Jesus, the all-knowing, all-seeing God who made the universe, wasn't worried at all. He was safe and obeying His heavenly Father in the temple. Whether we are lost or scared, we can cry out to God. He is the One who is in control. He knows our hearts, our fears, and where we are at every moment. We can rest in Him in even the scariest of moments.

Written by Krista | FROM POLAND AND CANADA

26

JOHN THE BAPTIST AND JESUS' BAPTISM

Like you, Jesus had a family. Of course, you already know about His mother, Mary, and earthly father, Joseph. But did you know Jesus had brothers and sisters, aunts and uncles, and a cousin? His cousin's name was John.

Now, John was a little odd. He lived in the desert, wore clothes made of camel hair, and ate grasshoppers and honey. (Let's just say John was *not* a picky eater.) But most importantly, John loved God with all his heart.

God had a special purpose for John's life. John was to prepare the people for the coming of their long-awaited Rescuer. John loved God so much that all he wanted to do was tell everyone about God. "Repent and be baptized!" John would call out to people. After a while, some began calling him "John the Baptist."

People began to come from all over to hear John talk about God and their need for Him. And as the crowds listened to John, they learned about their sins and their need for a Rescuer. Many repented and wanted to be baptized. They were sorry for the wrong things they had done and wanted their sins washed away so that they could start a new life with God. Lines of people would form alongside the Jordan River, and John would baptize each and every person there.

Then one day, something truly amazing happened. As John was baptizing people in the Jordan River, his cousin Jesus came to be baptized. John was surprised to see Jesus, for he knew that Jesus had never done anything wrong. (Can you imagine *never* doing *anything* wrong in your life?) Jesus was sinless, so He didn't need to be baptized.

"Look!" John said to everyone along the river waiting to be baptized. **"The Lamb of God, who takes away the sins of the world, is here!"**

As Jesus stepped into the calm, warm water and waded over to John, He said, "John, I want you to baptize Me too."

"But who am I to baptize You?" John replied, his voice filled with humility. "You are sinless. I am not worthy of such an honor. You should be baptizing me instead."

"It's what God wants Me to do, John. I must obey God," Jesus replied, smiling at John.

At that moment, John understood, so he baptized his cousin, the long-awaited Rescuer.

As Jesus rose out of the water, the most wonderful thing happened. Heaven opened up, as if a curtain were pulled back in the sky. The beauty of heaven filled the clouds. Then the Holy Spirit flew down from heaven in the form of a dove and rested on Jesus. And with it came the strongest, most loving, and most wonderful voice from heaven.

"This is My Son. I love Him with all My heart, and I am very proud of Him. Listen to Him," said God.

At that moment, God was a proud Dad, blessing His Son with powerful words of praise for all to hear. The same voice that spoke the world into existence also spoke words of praise as His Son began His rescue mission.

Dear God, thank You for sending Jesus to show us how to live. Please help me live in a way that pleases You. I pray that people all over the world will come to know You and that there would be peace. Amen.

Prayer by Michael | FROM THE UNITED STATES OF AMERICA

Thoughts from Around the World

When I was a little girl, I remember how bumpy the road into our town was. We would ride the bus, and it would shake because the road was so rough. The road was filled with rocks and had many curves. But many years later, someone fixed it by removing the rocks and making the street flat and straight. Now, traveling on that road has become so easy.

John the Baptist was called to prepare the way for the Lord and make a straight path for Him (Mark 1:2–3). Before they were baptized, John would ask the people to first repent and then live in ways that would show they had repented.

So how can we prepare the way for the Lord? If we want Jesus to walk into our lives, we should prepare our hearts (the way) for Him by repenting, which means confessing that we are sinners, deciding to stop living for our own desires, and daily choosing to live in a way that honors God. We can't do it on our own, but when Jesus, the Son of God, comes into our hearts, the Holy Spirit will also come and walk with us, helping us every minute of our lives.

Written by Wafa | FROM JORDAN

27

JESUS IN THE DESERT

MATTHEW 4:1–11; LUKE 4:1–13

After Jesus was baptized, He entered the desert. Jesus' rescue mission, which had been planned from the beginning of time, was about to begin. But first He needed to prepare for the mission by spending time alone with God.

In the desert, Jesus didn't eat anything for forty days and forty nights. Instead, He took time to pray and focus on what was ahead. Jesus knew that from the moment sin entered the world in the garden of Eden, the war between good and evil had begun. He knew the path before Him and the price He would have to pay for our sin.

At the end of the forty days, when Jesus' physical body was feeling its weakest from hunger, Satan came to tempt Him.

"If You are truly God's Son, then prove it," Satan hissed. "I see You're hungry. Why don't You turn these hard stones into delicious, soft bread to feed Yourself?"

Jesus replied, "It is written in the Scriptures, 'We do not live on only bread but on everything God says.'"

Seeing that he couldn't tempt Jesus to disobey God due to His hunger, Satan decided to tempt Jesus another way by offering Him power over the entire world, if Jesus would worship him just once.

Again, Jesus replied to Satan's lies, "It is written that we should only worship and serve God."

Frustrated, Satan tried to trick Jesus a third time. This time, Satan brought Jesus to the tallest spot on the temple. "If You're really God's Son, then prove it. Jump off this high building and see if God's angels will come and protect You."

But Jesus replied, "It is written, 'Don't put God to the test.'"

Defeated, Satan left Jesus alone. Unlike Adam and Eve with the serpent in the garden of Eden, Jesus had successfully resisted temptation. Though Satan tried to tempt Jesus three different times in three different ways, Jesus knew who He was and what He needed to do. Jesus knew God loved Him, and He knew God loved the world, and for the great rescue mission to take place, Jesus needed to walk forward in obedience and trust God each step of the way.

Jesus, please show me what is wrong and teach me to say no to things that are bad and make You sad. Amen.

Prayer by Júlia | FROM BRAZIL

Thoughts from Around the World

Satan wants us to disobey God. The Bible says he comes only to steal, kill, and destroy. He is always thinking of ways to take us away from God. He is a powerful enemy, but the good news is that he is not more powerful than God! Jesus showed us how to defeat Satan. We do this by saying no and speaking the truth of God's Word. Three times Satan told Jesus to do something, and each time Jesus said no to Satan and responded with Scripture. Jesus Himself promised that if we submit to God and resist the devil, he will flee from us (James 4:7). So, the next time you have an idea or a desire to do something that you know will break God's law and bring Him sadness, do like Jesus. Remember God's Word, say no, and put the devil on the run.

Written by Phoenix Maria | FROM BRAZIL

28

CHOOSING THE TWELVE DISCIPLES

MATTHEW 4:18–22

After Jesus resisted Satan's temptations in the desert, He set out on His rescue mission. He had a lot to do in a short amount of time, and He knew He didn't want to do it all alone. So Jesus invited some friends to join Him. Jesus knew that life is always better when you invite others to join you on the journey.

Now, you'd probably think Jesus would want the smartest, richest, best-looking friends to help Him, right? Wrong. **It doesn't matter to Jesus if you're rich or poor, tall or short, from one area of the world or another. What matters most to Jesus is your heart.** The world may value your worth by what you look like on the outside or what special skills you may have, but Jesus isn't like that. He knows your value and worth come from God, and in His eyes, you are priceless.

Art by Hanelle | FROM KENYA

So one day, as Jesus was walking by the Sea of Galilee, He looked off into the distance and saw two brothers, Peter and Andrew, fishing on the sea. Jesus cupped His hands around His mouth and called out to the brothers. The sound of His voice effortlessly carried across the water. "Come follow Me!" He yelled. "Today you are fishing for fish, but one day you will be fishers of men."

And right away Peter and Andrew left what they were doing and followed Jesus.

A little while later, Jesus saw two more brothers, James and John, who were also fishermen. Jesus asked them to join Him too. In all, Jesus asked twelve different men

to join Him as His disciples on His exciting rescue mission, a mission that would change the world forever and change people's lives for eternity. These were ordinary men, doing ordinary jobs like being fishermen. But when Jesus called out to them, they had faith in Jesus and responded, "Yes!" They didn't exactly know what they were saying yes to, but from the moment they met Jesus, they knew they never wanted to leave His side.

Jesus, thank You for keeping me safe as I live as Your disciple every day. Thank You for choosing me just as I am. Amen.

Prayer by Hanelle | FROM KENYA

Thoughts from Around the World

When you are struggling with a project, what's your next step? How do you move forward? You ask a teacher or a parent for help. They have the knowledge and skill to guide you to the right answer or can show you how to begin. When you ask different people with different skills for help, you can accomplish more than you could by yourself.

Jesus had an important project to do, and He picked people who could help Him with the project. Those who were willing joined Him. Today, everyone is welcome in Jesus' mission, whether they are short or tall, or if they play football or like swimming. Everyone is invited to join Jesus in the mission.

Written by Janet | FROM KENYA

137

29

SERMON ON THE MOUNT

MATTHEW 5–7

Jesus went from town to town with the twelve disciples, telling people about God. When Jesus spoke, what amazed people most was how He talked about God with authority.

Many people came to Jesus to be healed of physical illnesses and disabilities, and Jesus was happy to help them. But Jesus' rescue mission was much bigger than helping and healing people physically. **He wanted to heal their hearts.**

When Jesus came to a town, crowds would come to hear what He had to say. Older people, young people, healthy people, sick people, men, women, children— they all wanted to hear more and learn more from Jesus.

One day Jesus gave one of His most famous sermons, which eventually became known as the Sermon on the Mount. As Jesus stood on a mountain with His twelve disciples, He looked around at all the people who had gathered to hear Him speak, and He had compassion on them. He knew many of them were worried about many things. Some were worried about what they would eat. Others were worried about what they would wear. Some struggled with hurting bodies and others with hurting hearts. Each of them had come to the mountainside that day for hope.

So Jesus sat down and began to speak. His words comforted and challenged all who listened.

"You are the light of the world," Jesus said. "When it's dark, people don't hide their light under a basket so they can't see it. They keep their light out so they can see everything around them! So don't try to hide your light by dimming it or putting it under a basket. Let your light shine so others can see the difference God makes in your life and praise Him for it.

"In this life, you will have enemies. But don't worry, because I do too. Instead of hating your enemies, I want you to love them. I know that can be really hard to do, so praying for them is a great place to start.

"And I know many of you are worrying about what you will eat and what you will wear. When you think about your future, you might feel scared and sick to your stomach, not knowing what tomorrow will be like. But I don't want you to worry. The next time your mind fills up with worries, I want you to pause and look at the birds outside your window and the beautiful flowers covering the fields. God always makes sure those birds are fed and those flowers can grow, so just imagine how much more important it is to Him that you are fed and taken care of. You mean so much more to God than birds or fields of flowers. So do not worry. Trust that God knows your needs and will take care of you. Instead of spending your days worrying about what

Art by Nolan | FROM THE UNITED STATES OF AMERICA

140

tomorrow will bring, spend your precious days serving God and obeying Him out of your love for Him."

As Jesus taught the crowd around Him, their hearts were filled with hope and their minds with greater understanding. When people looked at Jesus and listened to what He had to say, they felt like God was speaking directly to them—because He was.

God, please take care of me and my friends the way You take care of the birds and the flowers. You are good! Amen.

Prayer by Nolan | FROM THE UNITED STATES OF AMERICA

Thoughts from Around the World

What's your father like? Is he kind? Harsh? Does he show up at your games or your recitals? Or maybe, for some reason, he's not been in your life. My dad died when I was a teenager, and although I miss him, I have a heavenly Father who absolutely amazes me with His love and care!

When Jesus spoke to the people on the mountain, He had an assignment for them. He wanted them to be the light in this dark world.

In Matthew 7:9–11, Jesus said, "Which of you, if your son asks for bread, will give him a stone? Or if he asks for a fish, will give him a snake? If you, then, though you are evil, know how to give good gifts to your children, how much more will your Father in heaven give good gifts to those who ask him!" (NIV).

We are never a bother to God, our Father. He wants to take care of your worries and meet your needs and wants you to be a light to this needy world. He is happy to help!

Written by Whitney | FROM THE UNITED STATES OF AMERICA

30

JESUS FEEDS THE FIVE THOUSAND

MATTHEW 14:13–21; MARK 6:30–44;
LUKE 9:10–17; JOHN 6:1–15

One day, Jesus decided it was time to get away with His disciples and take a break. So Jesus and His disciples got on a boat to sail across to the other side of the lake. But to the disciples' surprise, the crowds of people found out where they were going and met them on the other side of the lake!

You see, people followed Jesus everywhere. Many people went to Jesus to be healed of their diseases or watch Him perform miracles. And when Jesus spoke, the people felt like they could listen to Him all day, and that day that's exactly what they did.

All the men, women, and children were captivated with what Jesus was teaching them. They felt like they could listen for days . . . until later in the evening, when their bellies started to rumble. The people had been listening to Jesus for hours, and they had forgotten to eat!

It was getting late, and there was nowhere to get food. The crowd was massive, and the men alone totaled five thousand—that's not counting all the women and children there too!

The disciples found themselves in a situation. What should they do? How could they get all these people fed? The disciples were worried. A few of them suggested sending everyone to nearby villages. The disciples didn't have enough money to buy food for everyone, and even if they did, where would they get the food at this time of day? The situation seemed impossible.

But was it?

Remember, with God nothing is impossible. But the disciples had forgotten who was with them. They had already seen Jesus perform many miracles, but in this moment they could only see the large number of people in front of them.

Finally one of the disciples, Andrew, came to Jesus and said, "I've found a young boy who has five loaves of bread and two fish he is willing to give us. But what good will so little food do for so many people?"

Then Jesus turned to look at the crowd in front of Him and asked them to sit down on the grass. Jesus was going to show them He was powerful enough to meet their spiritual *and* physical needs. All day long He had been filling up their hearts with what He was teaching them. Now He was going to show them He was powerful enough to fill their tummies too.

Jesus took what the boy gave Him, looked up into heaven, and thanked God for the food. Then He took the five loaves and two fish—all that the boy gave—and made it enough. More than enough, actually. Jesus started dividing up the food, giving it to the disciples to feed the crowd. Each person who reached into the baskets for food had more than enough to eat! The thousands of people were fed until their tummies were full. Not only was there enough food to go around from that boy's gift of five loaves and two fish, but there were twelve whole baskets of food left over!

Jesus filled the people's tummies. But He also showed that when people, even young boys and girls, give Jesus what they have—even if what they have doesn't seem like it will make a difference—it is always enough.

Art by Nathalia | FROM FRANCE

A miracle happened that day on the side of that hill, as thousands of hungry people were given food that did not run out. Jesus is a master of making something out of nothing. He's been doing it since the beginning of time. That day the disciples and that crowd of people learned that nothing is impossible in His capable hands.

Dear God, I thank You for all that I have in my hands. I ask You to take it to bless others. Amen.

Prayer by Nathalia | FROM FRANCE

Thoughts from Around the World

"Will this be enough for everyone?"

Jesus was with His disciples at the Sea of Galilee, and many people were coming to listen to Him because they saw His miracles. In the evening Jesus asked His disciples if they could give them something to eat, but no one had anything. But there was a boy with five loaves of bread and two fish. He shared all he had and offered it to the disciples. The men did not think this was enough, but Jesus took the loaves and prayed to His Father. And when He finished, what seemed so little was enough for everyone, to the point that the disciples collected twelve baskets of food that had been left over.

Sometimes what we have in our hands seems little. But when we give what we have to Jesus, it is much. And it can be a blessing for many people.

What do you have in your hands for Jesus? Would you share it?

Written by Elena | FROM FRANCE

31

JESUS LOVES THE LITTLE CHILDREN

MATTHEW 19:13–15; MARK 10:13–16

The disciples were with Jesus every single day, watching Him perform miracle after miracle right in front of their eyes. But sometimes they still forgot about their true mission.

One day, some parents brought their children to see Jesus. They knew Jesus had the power to bless their children. But as the children approached Jesus, the disciples told them Jesus was too busy. They even scolded the parents for bothering them with their children!

Jesus saw the disciples talking angrily with the parents. And He knew it was time to teach another important lesson.

"Always let the little children come to Me," Jesus told His disciples. "Never, ever stop them! I always have time for children. They are so important to Me. And they should be important to you too, because children have something to teach you. Truthfully, the kingdom of God belongs to people who are like these children. Children are trusting. Their hearts are open and accepting, and they are quick to have faith. To enter the kingdom of God, you should be like these little children."

Art by Derrick | FROM RWANDA

Then Jesus took the children into His arms. He put His hands on the little ones and blessed them. The disciples stood nearby, watching. But this time they were quiet, contemplating the important lesson their Savior had taught them: that Jesus loves every single child so very much.

Thank You for letting us learn about Jesus and how He loves and welcomes children. Please open our hearts to learn what else You want to teach us. Help us to be brave and follow You, knowing that You are always with us. And please help us to be humble and serve You out of our love for You. Amen.

Prayer by Derrick | FROM RWANDA

Thoughts from Around the World

In my village, many people don't listen to younger kids while they share their thoughts or Bible knowledge. That's not a good thing to do, because kids also can share knowledge with older people. Jesus teaches about the importance of humility and a childlike faith to enter the kingdom of heaven. Jesus emphasizes the value of children, stating that "the kingdom of heaven belongs to such as these" (Matthew 19:14 NIV). He also demonstrates the significance of compassion and inclusivity, welcoming the children and blessing them despite societal norms or expectations. This story encourages people to embrace humility, openness, and trust in God, recognizing that these qualities are essential for entering into a relationship with God and experiencing His kingdom.

Written by Stephanie | FROM RWANDA

32

PARABLE OF THE PRODIGAL SON

LUKE 15:11–32

When Jesus taught people about God, He often told stories to help them understand what God is like. One of His most famous stories is about a father and his two sons.

Now, this father was wealthy. The older son was obedient and did what his father asked, but the younger son didn't like to be told what to do. The younger son couldn't wait to get away from the rules of his father and live the way he wanted.

Eventually, the younger son went to his father and asked for his inheritance. This was a sum of money he wasn't supposed to receive for many years. The father was sad but agreed to give his son what he wanted. Immediately the young man took the money and left his family.

Finally, I can do what I want! the young man thought. *No more rules for me! From now on I'll be on my own, and I'll be happy.* And he was for a while. He traveled where he wanted and bought whatever his heart desired. Everything was going great . . . until the money ran out. Soon the traveling stopped, and his friends left him. Before long he didn't even have a place to live.

To make matters worse, around that time a famine hit the country, and the young man decided to get a job so he could buy something to eat. But the only job he could find was taking care of a farmer's pigs. Not only was the job messy, stinky, and unpleasant, but also it didn't pay very much. Soon the young man found himself getting hungrier and hungrier. Eventually, he got so hungry that he wanted to eat the slop the pigs were eating. Yuck!

Then the young man started thinking about his home. *At home, the people who work for my dad always have good food to eat. They are taken care of and always have a place to live,* he thought to himself. *What a mistake I've made! Now I see how good I had it in my father's house. If my dad saw me now, he would be so disappointed in me.*

But I can't stay here any longer. I have to go back home! I can't expect my dad to forgive me and welcome me back home as his son. But maybe, just maybe, he'll let me work for him like his other workers.

So the younger son left the pigsty and headed back home.

As the son neared his home, he grew nervous. *What will my dad think of me? Will he even want to see me?* the son thought. Fear squeezed his heart, and he was tempted to turn back around, fearing the rejection he was sure he would receive.

The young man's father saw his son far in the distance. Without hesitation, the father began to run toward his son with love and joy in his heart.

As the father reached his son, the young man was overcome with regret. "Father, I have made so many bad choices. I have messed up so many times that I know you

Art by Avigeya | FROM UKRAINE

can never forgive me." But to the young man's surprise, he couldn't get out all the words he had rehearsed on his way home. Because, with tears in his eyes, his father had pulled him into his strong, loving arms and squeezed tight.

"Hurry!" the father said to his servants. "Bring my best robe and put it on my son. Put a special ring on his finger. Give him sandals to wear. We'll have a feast and a party, for my son was lost but now is found!"

The father took the young man home. The pain and mistakes were in the past. This was a day of forgiveness and celebration!

Jesus told this story so the people listening would know that no matter how far they strayed from God, they could always go back to Him. No matter how much they sinned, no matter what bad choices they made, they could always find for-giveness in God. God is a loving Father who gives rules for His children to obey for their own good. But even when His children don't follow these rules perfectly, they are always welcomed back home when they are truly sorry, because God will always forgive those who return to Him and ask for forgiveness.

Thank You, God, for providing for me and for the parents who care for me. Thank You for accepting me and forgiving me when I make mistakes. Amen.

Prayer by Avigeya | FROM UKRAINE

Thoughts from Around the World

In my country, Ukraine, there was a time when the leaders said we didn't need God's rules. But without them, people started doing bad things. The people thought they wouldn't get in trouble because there were no more rules. Churches were closed, and people who believed in God were sometimes put in jail. Life became very hard because people didn't respect God.

Now, those bad days are over. Churches are open, and people can read the Bible and worship God together. Many people who didn't obey God before are now saying sorry and coming back to Him. They feel God's love in a special way. They know how bad life can be without God, and they are happy that God still loves them and welcomes them back, even after they made bad choices. We can learn from this that God always loves His children. God welcomes home anyone who asks for forgiveness. God cleans them up and throws a big party for them.

Written by Evgenia | FROM UKRAINE

33

THE LAST SUPPER

MATTHEW 26:17-30; MARK 14:12-26;
LUKE 22:7-38; JOHN 13:1-35

One special night, Jesus gathered His twelve disciples together to share the Passover meal. This meal was special because, as you might remember, it helped the Jewish people remember how God miraculously rescued them from being enslaved in the land of Egypt.

But this evening was like no other. God's rescue mission was in its final stages.

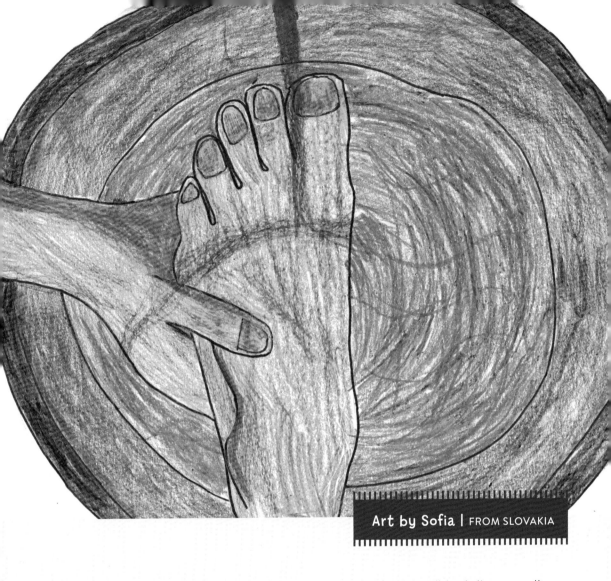

When the disciples sat down for the Passover meal, they all had dirty, smelly feet. Back then, everyone wore sandals. The streets they walked on were unpaved dirt and also used by animals. This made everyone's feet really dusty and gross. During the meal Jesus got up and grabbed a bowl and a towel. He got down on His knees and started washing the feet of every single disciple.

When Jesus came to wash Peter's feet, Peter protested, "You can't wash my feet, Jesus!" You see, even though Peter had watched Jesus humbly serve people, he still didn't understand Jesus' true rescue mission. Peter didn't understand that Jesus came to serve, not be served.

"Peter," Jesus said gently as He knelt down, "if you don't let Me wash your feet, then you aren't one of My people."

"If that is the case," Peter replied, "then wash my hands and head too!"

Then, after humbly and lovingly washing the disciples' feet, Jesus got up and took His place at the table. "Do you see what I have done?" He asked the disciples. "I am your teacher, yet I have washed your feet. Now I want you to follow My example and wash one another's feet too. **No person is better than another.** The greatest thing you can do is humbly serve one another out of love."

Then He made a startling announcement: "One of you has decided to betray Me."

The disciples were shocked at the news. *Who could it be?* they wondered.

The disciple Judas looked up and said, "Jesus, not me, is it?"

Jesus' eyes filled with sadness. "Yes," He said. "It's you."

Then to everyone's surprise, Judas got up and walked out of the room and into the darkness of the night.

After Judas left, Jesus picked up the freshly baked bread, broke off a piece for each of the remaining disciples, and gave it to them. "This bread is a symbol of My body, which will soon be broken for each of you," Jesus said.

Then He held up a cup of wine and said, "This wine is a symbol of My blood, which will soon be poured out for you. This is all a symbol of the new agreement that God is making with His people. **So whenever you do this, remember Me.** Tonight will be the last time I share the Passover meal with you. But don't worry, we will have it again when we are all in heaven together. I will not be with you much longer, so remember to love each other as I have loved you."

At that time, the disciples didn't really understand what Jesus was talking about, but they soon would. After dinner, Jesus led them out of the house into the night, and they walked together to a garden so Jesus could pray.

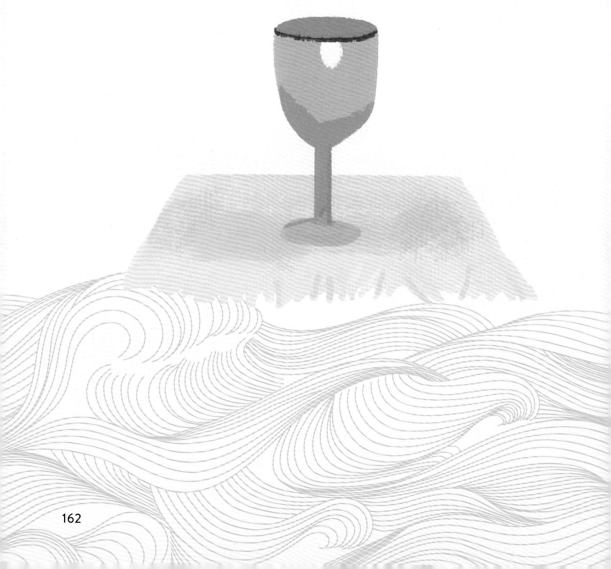

Dear God, please help me to love others just as You did, even when it's hard. Help me to serve others the way You did. Thank You for loving me no matter what. Amen.

Prayer by Sofia | FROM SLOVAKIA

Thoughts from Around the World

Just as we come together on special occasions, Jesus gathered His disciples and ate the Last Supper with them before accomplishing His rescue mission. During the meal, Jesus gave them the best example of how we should serve one another by washing their feet, which at that time was considered inferior work. Even today, many of us avoid doing such work for others and do not treat one another with humility and respect. But Jesus has commanded us to help and serve one another with love and affection, and He showed us how this should be done.

We are all part of Jesus' rescue mission. Today we want to help and serve one another by sharing His love and affection with everyone. Even if people consider us inferior, we must follow the path shown by Jesus through our behavior and character.

"For the Son of Man came to seek and to save the lost" (Luke 19:10 NIV).

Written by Bakhtawer | FROM PAKISTAN

163

34

THE GARDEN AND JESUS' ARREST

MATTHEW 26:36–68; MARK 14:32–52;
LUKE 22:39–53; JOHN 18:1–11

As Jesus and His disciples walked into the garden, the heaviness of what was coming cloaked Jesus like a thick blanket on a hot summer night. The weight seemed to drain Jesus' strength with each step He took forward.

The rescue mission was set in motion. But the path of obedience is not always easy. Many times people have to make sacrifices in order to obey. Jesus' path was no different.

Art by Hadassah | FROM MYANMAR

"My heart is filled with sorrow, and I need to pray to My Father," Jesus said to His disciples as they found an area of the garden to sit down. "I know it is late, and you all are tired, but please stay up with Me and keep watch."

"We will," the men responded. But soon they each grew tired and fell asleep.

Meanwhile, Jesus prayed. "Father, I love You and want to obey You. I know what I am about to do is necessary for this rescue mission. If there's any other way to do this, Father, please make a way. However, if this is how the mission needs to be carried out, I'll still do it. Your will be done, not Mine." Jesus prayed this three times.

Soon the darkness of the night gave way to the flicker of torches. The muffled voices of soldiers, along with their marching feet and clanging swords, grew louder. When Jesus saw the soldiers, He told the disciples to rise to their feet. The time for the mission had come.

Leading the soldiers was Judas, the disciple who had betrayed Jesus for thirty pieces of silver. He showed the soldiers who Jesus was by kissing Jesus on the cheek.

Peter looked on in disbelief as the soldiers grabbed Jesus and arrested Him. Soon Peter's disbelief was replaced by fear. He grabbed his sword and cut off the high priest's servant's ear—to defend Jesus.

"Put your sword away, Peter," Jesus said. "This battle cannot be fought with swords. **But trust Me: this is all part of the rescue plan I've been telling you about.** Don't you know I could call down thousands of angels to protect Me? But the Scriptures say it must happen this way." With that, Jesus touched the servant's ear and healed it.

Jesus was taken away like a criminal, even though He never had done anything wrong. And the disciples, who once had pledged their allegiance to Him, suddenly didn't feel very brave anymore. Fear overtook them, and they each ran away.

Jesus was left alone with no friends, only enemies.

The soldiers immediately took Jesus to the Jewish leaders. The Jewish leaders didn't like Jesus because the people loved Jesus. And because Jesus was more popular than the Jewish leaders, Jesus' presence threatened their power over the people. They were jealous. But what really made them hate Jesus and want to kill Him was when Jesus said He is the Son of God, which He is. Jesus had come to rescue the world from their sins. The only one who could do that was someone who was perfect, without sin, and that was Jesus.

"I hear that You think You're the Son of God," the high priest said to Jesus. Even though the high priest knew a lot about God from reading God's Word, he didn't understand who Jesus is or about Jesus' rescue mission. This shows that we can know a lot about God and yet not know God, even when He is standing right in front of us.

"Because You think You're the Son of God, You must die!" the Jewish leaders proclaimed. "You are no king of ours!" Then they spit on Him and hit Him with their fists. Then they led Jesus away.

Thank You, God, for this day. I'm thankful for Your sacrifice. You saved us even though You were sad about Your Son dying. In Jesus' name we pray, amen.

Prayer by Hadassah | FROM MYANMAR

Thoughts from Around the World

After the Last Supper, Jesus wanted His disciples to pray with Him, as His strength was drained and His heart was heavy. In the same way, Jesus wants us to pray, to talk to Him in our daily lives, so we will have strength to face difficulties.

When Jesus was arrested, He asked Peter to put his sword away because Jesus Himself is the healer, and He wants us to love our enemies. Sometimes our friends might do bad things to us or betray us, just as Judas betrayed Jesus. But Jesus wants us to forgive them as He forgave us.

Jesus is the Son of God, and He chose to save us from our sins. Because He never sinned, He took the shame for us and chose to die. One day, we will be with Him if we believe in Jesus as the Son of God. This is the beautiful story of God's plan for us.

Written by Moo Be | FROM MYANMAR

35

THE CRUCIFIXION

MATTHEW 27; MARK 15;
LUKE 23; JOHN 18:28–19:42

Early the next morning, the Jewish leaders brought Jesus to Pilate, the Roman ruler of the area. Pilate began to question Jesus.

"Are You the king of the Jews?" he asked.

"It is as you say," Jesus replied. Even though saying yes could get Him in trouble, Jesus still said yes because He knew this was all part of the rescue plan. No matter how painful the road of obedience was before Him, Jesus was committed to walking it.

But Pilate was no fool. He knew why the Jewish leaders wanted Jesus dead. They were jealous of Jesus, because many of their people were inspired by Him.

After asking Jesus questions over and over again, Pilate knew Jesus was innocent and wanted to release Him. But the Jewish leaders cried out for Jesus to be crucified. Pilate was surprised by their response, that they wanted to send an innocent person to die. Pilate offered to let one Jewish prisoner go and allow the crowd to choose who he would release. They could let Jesus, who was innocent, go or a dangerous man named Barabbas, who was a murderer. To Pilate's shock, the crowd wanted him to let Barabbas go, not Jesus.

Finally, Pilate had enough. He was more concerned with not making the crowd angry with him than he was with doing the right thing. "Fine," he said. "Have it your way." He ordered Roman soldiers to take Jesus away to be crucified, and Barabbas was given his freedom.

Immediately the soldiers began to beat Jesus and make fun of Him. "So You're the king of the Jews! Then You'll need a crown and a robe!" So they made a crown of thorns and pushed it down on Jesus' head, causing His head to bleed. Then after beating Him with a whip, they put a scar-

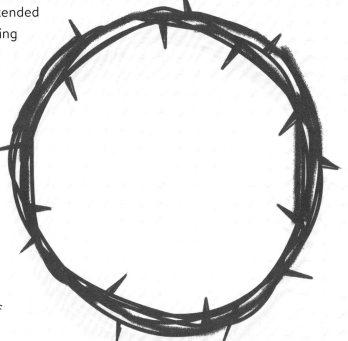

let robe on His back and pretended to bow down to Him. "Hail, king of the Jews!" they said and laughed, not knowing that Jesus is the King of kings and had come to rescue them too.

Then the soldiers led Jesus up a hill to crucify Him. At the top of the hill, they nailed Jesus to the cross and placed a sign above His head that read "The king of the Jews." On either side of Jesus were two criminals.

The Jewish leaders and soldiers began to yell at Jesus and make fun of Him as He hung on the cross, dying for their sins. "I thought You said You are the Son of God! If You are, then get down off that cross and save Yourself!" they screamed.

But it was true. Jesus is the Son of God. He could have come down off the cross, but His love for you and me and the people of the world kept Him there. Coming down wasn't part of the rescue plan. Jesus had come to die so that others could live. And even though He was innocent, Jesus chose to sacrifice His perfect, sinless life so that everyone who accepts His gift of salvation can be rescued from the punishment of their sins and have eternal life.

With His body and heart full of pain, Jesus looked down at the crowd below. "Forgive them, Father. They don't know what they are doing. They don't understand who I am." And they didn't. They didn't realize that Jesus loved them and came to rescue them by dying for them. This was the only way they could be forgiven of their sins.

And then, with His last breath, Jesus said, "It is finished!" And it was.

In that moment, the earth responded with an earthquake. The sky became pitch black, even though it was in the middle of the day, and the earth trembled and the rocks split. It was as if the whole world were cracking open from the weight of sin Jesus had to bear. He had paid it all.

173

At that moment surely everything seemed wrong to the disciples. It probably felt as though good had not conquered evil, but instead evil had conquered good. They were devastated, scared, and confused when Jesus died. All their hopes and dreams for their ministry had died with Jesus on the cross, and they didn't know what to think. *Where did we go wrong?* they might have wondered. *We thought that He was the Messiah, the Rescuer. All those miracles, all the lives that had been helped and changed, what was it all for?*

Art by Brinnley | FROM THE UNITED STATES OF AMERICA

Finally, Jesus was taken off the cross and placed in a tomb carved out of rock. A massive stone, as tall as a human, was placed in front of the opening to the tomb, because the Jewish leaders wanted to make sure no one could go in or out of Jesus' tomb. They remembered Jesus had said He would come back to life after three days, and they didn't want to take any chances that someone could take His body and say He had risen from the dead. So they also had soldiers stand guard at Jesus' tomb, just in case.

But the rescue mission wasn't over.

Thank You for loving me so much that You died on the cross for my sins. That must have really hurt, and I'm so sorry You had to go through that. Thank You for giving me the best gift ever—the gift of being saved and having eternal life with You in heaven. I love You so much, Jesus. Amen.

Prayer by Brinnley | FROM THE UNITED STATES OF AMERICA

Thoughts from Around the World

We all do something wrong from time to time. We call that wrongdoing "sin." And sin separates us from God. But Jesus, God's Son, came to earth to take away our sin. Jesus knew that some people wouldn't believe that He is God and would punish Him, but He still decided to take up the cross. He gave His life so that everybody can be saved and one day live with God forever. All we need to do is believe that Jesus is God's Son and let Him know that we are sorry for the bad things we do. We welcome Him into our hearts because He is our Savior.

Written by Tanja | FROM GERMANY

36

THE RESURRECTION

MATTHEW 28:1–10; MARK 16:1–8;
LUKE 24:1–12; JOHN 20:1–18;
1 CORINTHIANS 15:6

Everyone who knew Jesus was heartbroken by His death. How could they go on without their dearest friend? Their lives were forever changed by Him, and now they couldn't think about their futures without feeling fearful.

The following day was no different. Just silence, heartache, and disbelief over what had taken place.

Then something magnificent happened. On Sunday, just as the sun was beginning to push back the darkness of the night, an earthquake shook the land. A mighty

angel, as bright as a bolt of lightning with clothing as white as fresh snow, came from heaven and rolled away the giant stone in front of the tomb! When the soldiers who were guarding Jesus' tomb saw the mighty angel, they froze in fear, unable to move.

As the first rays of dawn spilled over the hill, a group of women who were among Jesus' followers reached His tomb. To their surprise, the tomb was open! The giant rock that had closed the tomb had been moved, and a mighty angel sat on top of it!

With excitement in his eyes and a smile on his face, the angel said, "Don't be afraid. I know you came looking for Jesus. But He isn't here! **Just like He told you, He has risen from the dead!** Come and see for yourselves, then go and tell the disciples what you have seen."

The women could hardly believe it. They didn't know whether to laugh or cry, jump up and down, or run inside the tomb to see if it really was  empty. What wonderful, wonderful news! Hope rushed into their hurting hearts and pushed the darkness and dread away.

The women ran as fast as they could to tell the disciples what they had seen. Jesus was alive, and the tomb was empty, just as He had promised! But the news seemed too good to be true, and at first the disciples didn't believe the women. Two of the disciples, Peter and John, had to see the empty tomb for themselves.

Art by Yoshiya | FROM JAPAN

Soon after, Jesus appeared to the disciples multiple times, as well as more than five hundred other people. Many people believed, but even then, some doubted. Nevertheless, a new day had dawned. **Jesus had defeated death, and sin had lost its sting.** He truly is the Rescuer!

God, I pray that everyone will know Jesus. Amen.

Prayer by Yoshiya | FROM JAPAN

Thoughts from Around the World

Can you imagine how sad the women felt as they walked to the tomb? When Jesus died, they'd lost hope. But God sent an angel to share this news: "He has risen! Jesus is alive!"

People in my country of Japan can relate to feeling hopeless. In 2011, the Great East Japan Earthquake destroyed schools and homes and killed many people. At that time, many people also lost hope. But people came from all over Japan and even from around the world to help. Less than 1 percent of the people who live here in Japan believe in Jesus, but God loves each of us and sent people to help us after the disaster. Some Christian women formed an organization called the Nozomi Project (*nozomi* is the Japanese word for "hope"), which helped women rebuild their lives by giving them a place to create and sell beautiful jewelry made from pottery, teapots, rice bowls, and dishes that were broken in the earthquake. No matter how hopeless we may feel, our mighty God gives us hope!

Written by Rie | FROM JAPAN

37

JESUS APPEARS ON THE ROAD TO EMMAUS

LUKE 24:13-35; ISAIAH 53:5-12;
ACTS 2:31-36; 13:36-41

Word began to spread that Jesus had risen from the dead. But still, some of Jesus' followers had a hard time believing the news. It just sounded too good to be true.

The day Jesus arose, two of those followers were walking to a nearby town called Emmaus, about seven miles away from Jerusalem. As they left the city, they began to discuss all they had heard from the women at the tomb, who said Jesus was alive. But before long, another man joined them on their walk.

"What are you both talking about so passionately?" the stranger asked.

"Haven't you heard about everything that's happened in Jerusalem?" one of the men named Cleopas answered.

"What things?" the stranger replied.

"You don't know?" the two friends exclaimed. "We're talking about Jesus. He was crucified on Friday, and today some women that we know told us Jesus has risen from the dead. They went to His tomb this morning, and when they got there, a mighty angel was there. The angel rolled away the gigantic stone that had closed Jesus' tomb. Now the women are claiming that Jesus' body wasn't inside the tomb. **They say the angel told them He is alive, that Jesus has been raised from the dead!** But we are having such a hard time believing this could be true."

"Why do you find this so hard to believe?" the stranger said to them. "Don't the Scriptures talk about a future Rescuer? Didn't the Messiah have to suffer these things?"

Before long, the three travelers reached Emmaus. By now, it was nearly evening and growing dark outside, so the two men invited the stranger to stay with them and have dinner.

Right before they began to eat, the stranger took the bread they were about to eat, broke it, and blessed it—just like Jesus had done a few days before with His twelve disciples! Suddenly the eyes of the two friends were opened, and they recognized who the stranger was: Jesus! Then Jesus vanished right before their eyes.

Art by Janelle | FROM AUSTRALIA

The two friends were shocked. The women had been right all along! And even though it was evening, the men got up from the table and headed back to Jerusalem to tell the other disciples what they had experienced. **Jesus was indeed alive.** He had risen from the dead, just as He said He would!

Thank You, God, for sending Jesus to die on the cross for my sins and for raising Him up again so that we can live in heaven with You. Amen.

Prayer by Janelle | FROM AUSTRALIA

Thoughts from Around the World

What a gentle Redeemer we have. He fulfills all of His promises. He comes to us even when we are confused or don't understand what is going on, and He gently leads us to the truth.

I grew up in Kenya, and as a child I remember God would set clues for my heart to know and experience His love for me. Sometimes as I looked up at the sky, I would see cloud formations of Bible characters my dad and mum had told me about, like Abraham. God loves little children, and when we pray, He hears our prayers.

I'm so glad that Jesus is alive. Even now He knocks gently at the door of my heart to remind me that He loves me and wants to live forever with me in heaven. My Redeemer has a cool house with streets of gold for me. I want to see it, and I want to see you all there too.

Written by Manoti | FROM KENYA

38

THE BEGINNING OF THE CHURCH

MATTHEW 28:16–20; ACTS 1–2

After appearing to many people over a number of days, it was finally time for Jesus to go back to heaven and sit at the right hand of God. The disciples surely must have been sad to hear Jesus wasn't staying with them.

"I promise to always be with you, even to the very end," Jesus reassured them. "Now, listen: I am sending you on a mission. **Go and tell others about Me and what I have taught you.** And for now, stay in Jerusalem. God is going to send the Holy Spirit, who will help each of you while I'm gone."

Then an amazing thing happened right before the disciples' eyes. Jesus began to rise into the sky. The disciples watched in amazement for as long as they could. Finally, they couldn't see Jesus any longer as He was hidden by clouds. And just then, two angels appeared.

"What are you looking for?" the angels asked. "Jesus has gone to heaven. But don't worry! He will come back the same way you saw Him leave."

So the disciples obeyed and stayed in Jerusalem, just like Jesus told them to do.

A few weeks later, during a holiday known as Pentecost, the disciples and other followers of Jesus were together at the same home. Suddenly, a strong wind came out of nowhere and filled the room. Immediately, small candle-like flames appeared over each person's head, which showed the arrival of the Holy Spirit. Shocked at what was happening, the people started speaking to each other, but to their surprise they were each speaking a language they didn't know.

The disciples left the house and started sharing the good news about Jesus with people in the streets. The people hearing the good news were surprised because they could easily understand what these disciples were saying to them, even though they spoke different languages! Then Peter, one of the disciples, stood up and spoke to the large crowd that had gathered.

"Friends, what has happened was predicted long ago by the prophet Joel. Joel said that God would pour His Spirit upon all people. And listen! **God sent Jesus, His one and only Son, to die for your sins, and God has raised Him up.** Jesus is alive and is now in heaven with God. So repent and be baptized and you, too, will receive the Holy Spirit and be saved."

187

That day the church was born, and over three thousand people became followers of Jesus Christ, now known as "Christians." What started that day has continued ever since. Like a ripple in the water, the good news of Jesus Christ spread out from Jerusalem to other towns, countries, and eventually the whole world. Each time a Christian shares the good news about Jesus, the rescue mission that Jesus started continues forward, one person at a time.

God, I will always be grateful for what You did for us, because You protected me and sent Jesus to die for us. Amen.

Prayer by Danae | FROM MEXICO

Thoughts from Around the World

Has someone ever given you a special gift? As Jesus returned to heaven, He reminded His friends that God had promised to give them a gift: the Holy Spirit. The Holy Spirit would give them the power to share the good news to many more people. There would be times when things would get difficult, as some people would want to stop them, but the Holy Spirit would be with them and give them the courage to continue. As we are followers of Jesus, the precious gift of the Holy Spirit is also available to us. You and I are part of the important mission of sharing the good news of Jesus. Now it's your turn to share this good news with your friends! If you ever feel afraid, remember God is with you, and He will give you the courage to achieve your mission.

Written by Narda | FROM MEXICO

39

PAUL'S CONVERSION

ACTS 9:1-22; 22:1-21

More and more people were hearing about Jesus' rescue mission and how they could be forgiven for their sins and saved. The good news was spreading like wildfire, and many people were becoming Christians.

But some people were *not* happy about this—including the Jewish leaders. One of these Jewish leaders was named Saul, who also went by Paul, his Greek name. Like other Jewish leaders, Paul hated the Christians.

Now, Paul was a very smart man who had been taught by some of the wisest Jewish teachers. He also worked very hard to follow God's rules. He thought all his good works and all his knowledge about God made him good. But it didn't. Like many of the Jewish leaders, Paul didn't understand who Jesus was or His great rescue mission yet. All Paul knew was that Jesus was crucified for saying He was the Son of God, and now His followers were saying He was alive. And Paul thought they needed to be stopped. He put Christians in jail for talking about Jesus. **Paul had never met Jesus—but Jesus was about to change that.**

One day Paul was traveling to a town called Damascus to put Christians there in jail. While he was on the road, the strangest thing happened. A bright light, brighter than anything Paul had ever seen, flashed from the sky. The light was so bright that it startled him, and he fell to the ground.

Then Paul heard a loud voice. "Paul, why are you persecuting Me?"

Scared, Paul asked the voice, "Who are you?"

"I'm Jesus," the voice replied. "I want you to go to Damascus, just like you had planned. Once you reach the town, there is a special person I want you to meet. He will tell you what to do."

Shaken by what just happened, Paul started to get up. But as he did, he realized that even though his eyes were open, he couldn't see. The friends who had been traveling with him had to help him get to Damascus.

For three days, Paul couldn't see. He didn't eat or drink anything, and he prayed about all that had happened.

At the same time Paul was sitting in darkness and praying, Jesus appeared in a dream to a Christian in that town named Ananias.

"Ananias," Jesus said in the dream, "I want you to go to a man named Paul. He has just arrived in your town, and right now he is blind. I want you to go to him and lay hands on him so he will see again."

But Ananias became scared. "Jesus, I have heard about Paul," Ananias answered. "He hates Christians and is throwing them in jail because he wants them to stop telling others about You."

"I have chosen Paul for a very important mission," Jesus said. "I want him to tell others about Me."

Ananias didn't question Jesus again. He obeyed Him and went to Paul.

"Hello, Brother Paul," Ananias said as he greeted the blind man. "Jesus spoke to me in my dream last night. He told me to come to you and lay hands on you, so that you will once again be able to see and be filled with the Holy Spirit."

Immediately after Ananias said this, scales fell from Paul's eyes, and he could see again. **And yet, everything looked different.** Paul no longer saw the world the same way he did before he met Jesus on the road to Damascus. Paul was now a new man with a new heart and a new purpose.

Art by Rose | FROM NORTHERN IRELAND

Paul was ready to play his part in the beautiful rescue mission Jesus had started. He would go on to spend the rest of his life telling others, from all walks of life, about Jesus. Paul preached the good news to Jews and Gentiles alike. He shared that it didn't matter how much you knew or didn't know. It didn't matter how good or bad you were. None of this mattered because Jesus died for you—and He loves you. You don't have to work to earn God's love. Anyone who repents and believes in Jesus will be saved. And that's all that really matters.

Heavenly Father, thank You for loving us so much that You sent Your only Son, Jesus, to die and give us new life. Thank You for helping us change completely like You did with Paul. Amen.

Prayer by Rose | FROM NORTHERN IRELAND

Thoughts from Around the World

This story tells us how a man who set out to attack followers of Jesus had an amazing encounter with Jesus. It changed his life. This man, Paul, was making life tough for God's people. He needed to be stopped in his tracks, and that's exactly what happened! Jesus met him on the road to Damascus, and after realizing who Jesus is, Paul made Jesus the Lord of his life. His old life was gone!

No matter what we have done in the past or how far we are from God, Jesus can stop us in our tracks, just as He did with Paul. We, too, can know Jesus personally as our Lord and Savior today.

Written by Pamela | FROM NORTHERN IRELAND

40

THE PROMISED RETURN OF CHRIST

REVELATION 1, 20–22

Jesus' disciples did just as Jesus had asked. They spent the rest of their lives traveling and telling people the good news—that salvation is found in Jesus and only in Jesus. He was and is the long-awaited Rescuer, who died for the sins of the world. And because of His sacrifice, anyone who accepts His free gift of salvation will be saved.

But many people hated this message of love, hope, and forgiveness. They wanted Jesus' disciples to stop preaching, so they did everything they could to stop them.

One of Jesus' disciples, John, was banished to an island as punishment for telling others about Jesus. But even banishment didn't stop John from obeying God.

One day when John was praying, Jesus appeared to him in a vision. "John, don't be afraid," He said. "I want you to write down what I'm about to show you."

Jesus showed John the future, a time that seemed far off and far away. John saw things he had never seen before, and he tried his best to describe what he saw. Some of the things John saw were bad and scary. Some were hard to understand, but he remembered Jesus' promise that He would be with us forever. **He would one day return to gather all the people who believed in Him and take them to be with Him in heaven.**

Art by Ava | FROM AUSTRALIA

At the end of the vision, Jesus showed John what heaven looks like. And heaven was more wonderful, more beautiful, and more magnificent than any words could describe! Everywhere John looked, everyone was happy. No more tears, no more fear, and no more sickness existed. Evil was gone because Jesus defeated Satan. **Heaven was pure, perfect, and beyond anyone's wildest imagination.**

Most importantly, it was a place where Jesus was ruling as the perfect King, forever. The rescue mission would finally be complete as God's people would be with Him and all would be made new.

At the end of the vision, Jesus said, "I'm coming soon. I am the beginning and the end, and I promise the best is yet to come! And I will give a great reward to each person who obeys Me. So for now, tell everyone to pray, 'Come, Lord Jesus, come.' And I promise I will! I am coming soon!"

Dear Jesus, I pray that all men, women, and children may know You and love You. And I ask that all would be saved. Amen.

Prayer by Ava | FROM AUSTRALIA

Thoughts from Around the World

We as Christians have our hope in the new heaven and the return of Christ. We are waiting for Him to come back and make everything right again. In this passage we see how Jesus will take us to a place called heaven, a city like no other, and only those who believe in Him will be there. God will be the only source of light, we will see the Tree of Life in the center of the city, and a river of fresh water will flow from the throne of God. There will be streets of pure gold and every type of gemstone.

Jesus will have the Book of Life with Him, the book where our names are written when we accept Him as our Lord and Savior and dedicate our lives to Him.

Don't you find it incredible that we will be hanging out with God forever?

Today, take some time to ask Jesus to help you tell your friends about this beautiful city that awaits all of us.

Written by Guisette | FROM AUSTRALIA

THE PATRIARCHS

2091 BC–1446 BC

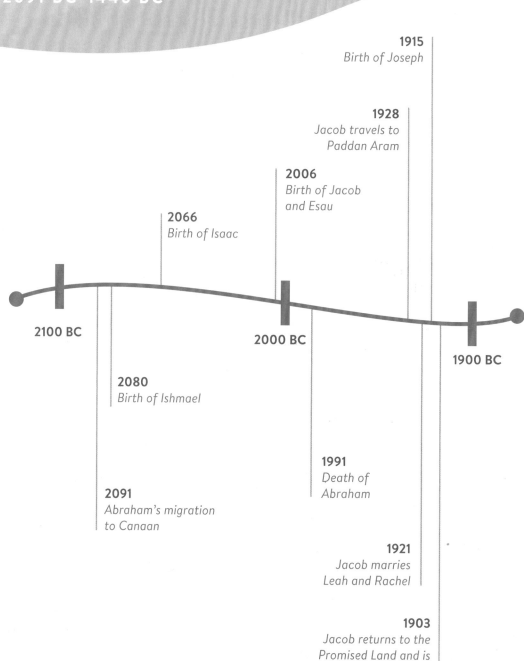

1915
Birth of Joseph

1928
*Jacob travels to
Paddan Aram*

2006
*Birth of Jacob
and Esau*

2066
Birth of Isaac

2100 BC

2000 BC

1900 BC

2080
Birth of Ishmael

2091
*Abraham's migration
to Canaan*

1991
*Death of
Abraham*

1921
*Jacob marries
Leah and Rachel*

1903
*Jacob returns to the
Promised Land and is
renamed Israel*

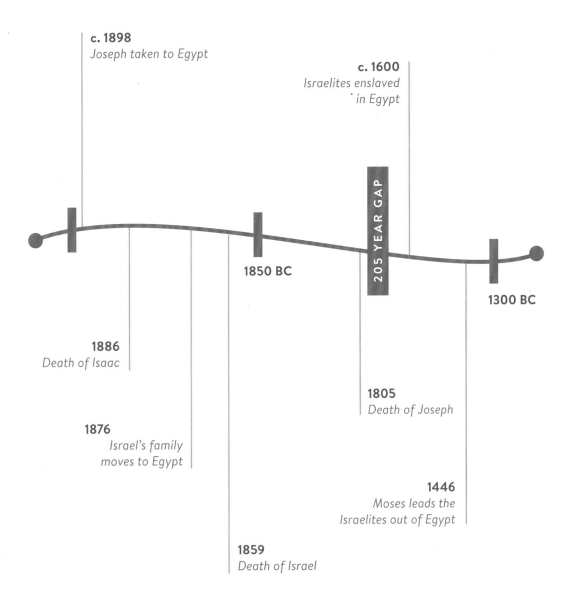

c. 1898
Joseph taken to Egypt

c. 1600
Israelites enslaved
in Egypt

205 YEAR GAP

1850 BC

1300 BC

1886
Death of Isaac

1805
Death of Joseph

1876
Israel's family
moves to Egypt

1446
Moses leads the
Israelites out of Egypt

1859
Death of Israel

JESUS' LIFE AND MINISTRY

5 BC–AD 33

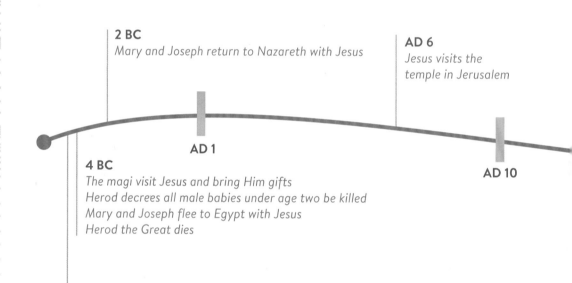

2 BC
Mary and Joseph return to Nazareth with Jesus

AD 6
*Jesus visits the
temple in Jerusalem*

AD 1

4 BC
The magi visit Jesus and bring Him gifts
Herod decrees all male babies under age two be killed
Mary and Joseph flee to Egypt with Jesus
Herod the Great dies

AD 10

5 BC
Jesus is born
An army of angels announce peace on earth
Mary and Joseph take Jesus to the temple to be dedicated

AD 32
Jesus is transfigured in glory
Jesus predicts His own death
Jesus heals a blind man

AD 30
Jesus cleanses the temple at the Passover festival
Jesus calls His remaining disciples
Jesus begins His ministry in Galilee
Jesus delivers the Sermon on the Mount
Jesus identifies Himself as the Messiah to a Samaritan woman
Jesus calms a storm on the Sea of Galilee
Jesus heals a bleeding woman and resurrects Jarius's daughter

AD 20

AD 29
John baptizes Jesus in the Jordan River
The devil tempts Jesus in the wilderness
Jesus calls His first disciples
Jesus turns water into wine

AD 30

AD 31
Jesus heals on the Sabbath
Jesus feeds 5,000 people
Jesus walks on water
Peter declares Jesus the Son of God

AD 33
Jesus raises Lazarus from the dead
Jesus rides triumphantly into Jerusalem
Jesus celebrates the Passover with His disciples
The Sanhedrin try Jesus, and Jesus is crucified
Jesus is resurrected
Jesus ascends to heaven and sits at the right hand of the Father
Jesus sends the Holy Spirit to dwell in and among believers in every nation

MEET THE WRITERS

Ana

Country: Portugal
Native Language: Portuguese
Favorite Food: Duck rice
Find Ana's writing on page 59.

Bakhtawer

Country: Pakistan
Native Language: Urdu
Favorite Food: Biryani
Favorite Bible Verse: "For the Son of Man came to seek and to save the lost" (Luke 19:10).
Find Bakhtawer's writing on page 163.

Charissa

Country: The Netherlands
Native Language: Dutch
Favorite Food: Kale stew with smoked sausage
Favorite Bible Verse: "If we are unfaithful, he remains faithful, since he cannot deny himself" (2 Timothy 2:13).
Find Charissa's writing on page 31.

Ebos

Country: Nigeria
Native Language: Hausa
Favorite Food: Plantain
Favorite Bible Verse: "God has declared one principle; two principles I have heard: God is strong" (Psalm 62:11).
Find Ebos's writing on page 63.

Elena

Country: France
Native Language: Spanish
Favorite Food: Arepas
Favorite Bible Verse: "I am the vine; you are the branches. The one who remains in me—and I in him—bears much fruit, because apart from me you can accomplish nothing" (John 15:5).
Find Elena's writing on page 147.

Evgenia

Country: Ukraine
Native Language: Ukrainian
Favorite Food: Borscht
Find Evgenia's writing on page 157.

Gail

Country: Kenya
Native Language: Luo
Favorite Food: Fish and ugali
Favorite Bible Verse: "For this is the way God loved the world: He gave his one and only Son, so that everyone who believes in him will not perish but have eternal life" (John 3:16).
Find Gail's writing on page 9.

Giovanna

Country: Brazil
Native Language: Portuguese
Favorite Food: Feijoada

Favorite Bible Verse: "As for you, the one who lives in the shelter of the Most High, and resides in the protective shadow of the Sovereign One— I say this about the LORD, my shelter and my stronghold, my God in whom I trust" (Psalm 91:1–2).

Find Giovanna's writing on page 13.

Gloria

Country: Italy

Native Language: Italian

Favorite Food: Pizza

Favorite Bible Verse: "'For I know what I have planned for you,' says the LORD. 'I have plans to prosper you, not to harm you. I have plans to give you a future filled with hope'" (Jeremiah 29:11).

Find Gloria's writing on page 117.

Guisette

Country: Australia

Native Language: Spanish

Favorite Food: Empanadas

Favorite Bible Verse: "'For I know what I have planned for you,' says the LORD. 'I have plans to prosper you, not to harm you. I have plans to give you a future filled with hope'" (Jeremiah 29:11).

Find Guisette's writing on page 199.

Irene

Country: Greece

Native Language: Greek

Favorite Food: Souvlaki

Favorite Bible Verse: "Jesus looked at them and replied, 'This is impossible for mere humans, but for God all things are possible'" (Matthew 19:26).

Find Irene's writing on page 23.

Janet

Country: Kenya

Native Language: Swahili

Favorite Food: Ugali

Favorite Bible Verse: "Now to him who by the power that is working within us is able to do far beyond all that we ask or think" (Ephesians 3:20).

Find Janet's writing on page 137.

Karina

Country: Kazakhstan

Native Language: Russian

Favorite Food: Dumplings with beef and pumpkin filling (manti)

Favorite Bible Verse: "Your word is a lamp to walk by, and a light to illumine my path" (Psalm 119:105).

Find Karina's writing on page 67.

Krista

Countries: Poland and Canada

Native Language: English

Favorite Food: Pierogi

Favorite Bible Verse: "By faith Abraham obeyed when he was called to go out to a place he would later receive as an inheritance, and he went out without understanding where he was going" (Hebrews 11:8).

Find Krista's writing on pages 5 and 125.

Manoti

Countries: Lives in Australia and is from Kenya

Native Language: Swahili

Favorite Foods: Chapati and dengu

Favorite Bible Verse: "This is the confidence that we have before him: that whenever we ask anything according to his will, he hears us. And if we know that he hears us in regard to whatever we ask, then we know that we have the requests that we have asked from him" (1 John 5:14–15).

Find Manoti's writing on page 183.

Moo Be

Country: Myanmar

Find Moo Be's writing on page 169.

Morta

Country: Lithuania

Native Language: Lithuanian

Favorite Food: Šaltibarščiai

Favorite Bible Verse: "For the scripture says, 'Everyone who believes in him will not be put to shame'" (Romans 10:11).

Find Morta's writing on page 87.

Narda

Country: Mexico

Native Language: Spanish

Favorite Food: Pozole

Favorite Bible Verse: "Then one of the elders said to me, 'Stop weeping! Look, the Lion of the tribe of Judah, the root of David, has conquered; thus he can open the scroll and its seven seals'" (Revelation 5:5).

Find Narda's writing on page 189.

Pamela

Country: Northern Ireland

Find Pamela's writing on page 195.

Petra

Country: Czech Republic

Native Language: Czech

Favorite Food: Štrůdl (apple strudel)

Favorite Bible Verse: "He says, 'Stop your striving and recognize that I am God. I will be exalted over the nations! I will be exalted over the earth!'" (Psalm 46:10).

Find Petra's writing on page 27.

Phoenix Maria

Country: Brazil

Native Language: Portuguese

Favorite Food: Farofa de banana

Favorite Bible Verse: "And we know that all things work together for good for those who love God, who are called according to his purpose" (Romans 8:28).

Find Phoenix Maria's writing on pages 109 and 133.

Rachel

Country: United States of America

Native Language: English

Favorite Food: Ice cream

Favorite Bible Verse: "Aren't two sparrows sold for a penny? Yet not one of them falls to the ground apart from your Father's will. Even all the hairs on your head are numbered. So do not be afraid; you are more valuable than many sparrows" (Matthew 10:29–31).

Find Rachel's writing on page 19.

Rie

Country: Japan
Native Language: Japanese
Favorite Food: Tempura
Favorite Bible Verse: "Always rejoice, constantly pray, in everything give thanks. For this is God's will for you in Christ Jesus" (1 Thessalonians 5:16–18).

Find Rie's writing on page 179.

Stella

Country: Kenya
Native Language: Swahili
Favorite Food: Pilau
Favorite Bible Verse: "So submit to God. But resist the devil and he will flee from you. Draw near to God and he will draw near to you. Cleanse your hands, you sinners, and make your hearts pure, you double-minded" (James 4:7–8).

Find Stella's writing on page 93.

Stephanie

Country: Rwanda
Native Language: Kinyarwanda
Favorite Food: Mixture of beans and bananas, our local food
Favorite Bible Verse: "And we know that all things work together for good for those who love God, who are called according to his purpose" (Romans 8:28).

Find Stephanie's writing on page 151.

Sylvia

Country: Uganda
Native Language: Luganda
Favorite Food: Matooke and fish with gnut paste
Favorite Bible Verse: "'For I know what I have planned for you,' says the LORD. 'I have plans to prosper you, not to harm you. I have plans to give you a future filled with hope'" (Jeremiah 29:11).

Find Sylvia's writing on page 49.

Tanja

Countries: Lives in Germany and is from Macedonia
Native Language: German
Favorite Food: Lasagna

Find Tanja's writing on page 175.

Vicky

Countries: United States of America and Thailand
Native Language: English
Favorite Food: Mango with sticky rice
Favorite Bible Verse: "Every wise woman has built her household, but a foolish woman tears it down with her own hands" (Proverbs 14:1).

Find Vicky's writing on pages 43 and 79.

Viola

Country: Hungary
Native Language: Hungarian
Favorite Food: Stuffed cabbage
Favorite Bible Verse: "But the wise will shine like the brightness of the heavenly expanse. And those bringing many to righteousness will be like the stars forever and ever" (Daniel 12:3).

Find Viola's writing on page 37.

Vivian

Country: China

Native Language: Chinese

Favorite Food: Sautéed tofu sheets with Anaheim pepper

Favorite Bible Verse: "Do not be conformed to this present world, but be transformed by the renewing of your mind, so that you may test and approve what is the will of God—what is good and well-pleasing and perfect" (Romans 12:2).

Find Vivian's writing on pages 83 and 121.

Wafa

Country: Jordan

Native Language: Arabic

Favorite Food: Mansaf

Favorite Bible Verse: "Now to him who by the power that is working within us is able to do far beyond all that we ask or think" (Ephesians 3:20).

Find Wafa's writing on page 129.

Whitney

Country: United States of America

Native Language: English

Favorite Food: Chicken and dumplings

Favorite Bible Verse: "I have told you these things so that in me you may have peace. In the world you have trouble and suffering, but take courage—I have conquered the world" (John 16:33).

Find Whitney's writing on page 141.

Yating

Country: Singapore

Native Languages: English and Chinese

Favorite Food: Fried tofu

Favorite Bible Verse: "I have asked the LORD for one thing—this is what I desire! I want to live in the LORD's house all the days of my life, so I can gaze at the splendor of the LORD and contemplate in his temple" (Psalm 27:4).

Find Yating's writing on page 97.

Zulay

Country: Colombia

Native Language: Spanish

Favorite Food: Arepa with cheese

Favorite Bible Verse: "For I am sure of this very thing, that the one who began a good work in you will perfect it until the day of Christ Jesus" (Philippians 1:6).

Find Zulay's writing on page 73 and 103.

MEET THE ARTISTS

Amanda

Country: Hungary

Native Language: Hungarian

Favorite Food: Lasagna

Favorite Activities: Crafting, drawing, and doing gymnastics

Favorite Bible Verse: "By casting all your cares on him because he cares for you" (1 Peter 5:7).

Find Amanda's artwork on page 34.

Anita

Country: Italy

Native Language: Italian

Favorite Food: Lasagna

Favorite Bible Verse: "I am able to do all things through the one who strengthens me" (Philippians 4:13).

Find Anita's artwork on page 116.

Ava

Country: United States of America

Native Language: English

Favorite Foods: Mac 'n' cheese and crayfish

Favorite Activity: Doing crafts and art

Favorite Bible Verse: "The second is: 'Love your neighbor as yourself.' There is no other commandment greater than these" (Mark 12:31).

Find Ava's artwork on page 15.

Ava

Country: Australia

Native Language: English

Favorite Food: Pizza

Favorite Activity: Playing with puppies

Favorite Bible Verse: "For this is the way God loved the world: He gave his one and only Son, so that everyone who believes in him will not perish but have eternal life" (John 3:16).

Find Ava's artwork on page 197.

Avigeya

Country: Ukraine

Native Language: Ukrainian

Favorite Food: Dumplings with potatoes

Favorite Activity: Artistic gymnastics

Favorite Bible Verse: "For this is the way God loved the world: He gave his one and only Son, so that everyone who believes in him will not perish but have eternal life" (John 3:16).

Find Avigeya's artwork on page 155.

Ben

Country: Kenya

Native Language: Samia

Favorite Food: Grilled pork

Favorite Activity: Skating

Favorite Bible Verse: "For everyone who calls on the name of the Lord will be saved" (Romans 10:13).

Find Ben's artwork on page 8.

Brinnley

Country: United States of America

Native Language: English

Favorite Food: Chick-fil-A spicy chicken deluxe sandwich

Favorite Activities: Playing tennis, rock climbing, making crafts, and playing with friends

Favorite Bible Verse: "You must love the LORD your God with your whole mind, your whole being, and all your strength" (Deuteronomy 6:5).

Find Brinnley's artwork on pages 119 and 174.

Danae

Country: Mexico

Native Language: Spanish

Favorite Food: Pozole

Favorite Activity: Drawing

Favorite Bible Verse: "For this is the way God loved the world: He gave his one and only Son, so that everyone who believes in him will not perish but have eternal life" (John 3:16).

Find Danae's artwork on page 188.

Derrick

Country: Rwanda

Native Language: Kinyarwanda

Favorite Foods: Roasted chicken and French fries

Favorite Activity: Playing football

Favorite Bible Verse: "Trust in the LORD with all your heart, and do not rely on your own understanding. Acknowledge him in all your ways, and he will make your paths straight" (Proverbs 3:5–6).

Find Derrick's artwork on page 150.

Elias

Countries: Poland and Canada

Native Languages: English and Polish

Favorite Food: Grits

Favorite Activity: Playing with LEGOs

Favorite Bible Verse: "The good person out of the good treasury of his heart produces good, and the evil person out of his evil treasury produces evil, for his mouth speaks from what fills his heart" (Luke 6:45).

Find Elias's artwork on page 3.

Elija

Country: Lithuania

Native Language: Lithuanian

Favorite Food: Varškėčiai

Favorite Era: Medieval

Favorite Bible Verse: "Don't be afraid, for I am with you. From the east I will bring your descendants; from the west I will gather you" (Isaiah 43:5).

Find Elija's artwork on page 85.

Ellie

Country: Taiwan

Native Language: Mandarin Chinese

Favorite Food: Honey soy barbecue chicken wings

Favorite Activity: Pretend play

Favorite Bible Verse: "And she gave birth to her firstborn son and wrapped him in strips of cloth and laid him in a manger, because there was no place for them in the inn" (Luke 2:7).

Find Ellie's artwork on page 81.

Evie

Country: United States of America

Native Language: English

Favorite Food: Dumplings

Favorite Bible Verse: "For this is the way God loved the world: He gave his one and only Son, so that everyone who believes in him will not perish but have eternal life" (John 3:16).

Find Evie's artwork on pages 95 and 97.

Hadassah

Country: Myanmar

Native Language: Karen

Favorite Food: Si htamin (yellow sticky rice)

Find Hadassah's artwork on page 165.

Hanelle

Country: Kenya

Native Language: Swahili

Favorite Food: Ugali and mchicha

Favorite Activity: Dancing

Favorite Bible Verse: "Then he said to his disciples, 'The harvest is plentiful, but the workers are few'" (Matthew 9:37).

Find Hanelle's artwork on page 135.

Helena

Country: Brazil

Native Language: Portuguese

Favorite Food: Arroz e feijão

Favorite Activity: Drawing

Favorite Bible Verse: "In the beginning God created the heavens and the earth" (Genesis 1:1).

Find Helena's artwork on pages 11 and 52.

Ian

Country: United States of America

Native Language: English

Favorite Food: Cheeseburgers

Favorite Activity: Building LEGOs

Favorite Bible Verse: "In my heart I store up your words, so I might not sin against you" (Psalm 119:11).

Find Ian's artwork on page 62.

Isabel

Country: Colombia

Native Language: Spanish

Favorite Food: Chicken rice

Favorite Bible Verse: "For this is the way God loved the world: He gave his one and only Son, so that everyone who believes in him will not perish but have eternal life" (John 3:16).

Find Isabel's artwork on pages 70 and 72.

Janelle

Country: Australia

Native Language: English

Favorite Food: Ugali

Favorite Activity: Swimming

Favorite Bible Verse: "The grace of the Lord Jesus Christ and the love of God and the fellowship of the Holy Spirit be with you all" (2 Corinthians 13:14 ESV).

Find Janelle's artwork on page 182.

Jonas

Countries: Poland and Canada

Native Languages: English and Polish

Favorite Food: French fries

Favorite Activity: Playing with my brothers

Favorite Bible Verse: "Do not be anxious about anything. Instead, in every situation, through prayer and petition with thanksgiving, tell your requests to God" (Philippians 4:6).

Find Jonas's artwork on page 123.

Júlia

Country: Brazil

Native Language: Portuguese

Favorite Food: Goiabada

Favorite Bible Verse: "The LORD strengthens and protects me; I trust in him with all my heart. I am rescued and my heart is full of joy; I will sing to him in gratitude" (Psalm 28:7).

Find Júlia's artwork on pages 107 and 132.

Lizz

Country: Colombia

Native Language: Spanish

Favorite Food: Arepa with cheese

Favorite Bible Verse: "O LORD, the king rejoices in the strength you give; he takes great delight in the deliverance you provide" (Psalm 21:1).

Find Lizz's artwork on page 102.

Mája

Country: Czech Republic

Native Language: Czech

Favorite Food: Goulash

Favorite Activity: Cooking

Favorite Bible Verse: "But I say to you, love your enemy and pray for those who persecute you, so that you may be like your Father in heaven, since he causes the sun to rise on the evil and the good, and sends rain on the righteous and the unrighteous" (Matthew 5:44–45).

Find Mája's artwork on page 25.

Michael

Countries: Lives in the United States of America, and his parents are from Jordan

Native Language: English

Favorite Food: Mloukhia

Favorite Activity: Playing soccer

Favorite Bible Verse: "Finally, be strengthened in the Lord and in the strength of his power. Clothe yourselves with the full armor of God, so that you will be able to stand against the schemes of the devil" (Ephesians 6:10–11).

Find Michael's artwork on page 128.

Nadya

Country: Ukraine

Native Language: Ukrainian

Favorite Food: Varenyky (potato dumplings)

Favorite Bible Verse: "And we know that all things work together for good for those who love God, who are called according to his purpose" (Romans 8:28).

Find Nadya's artwork on page 65.

Natalie

Countries: United States of America and Japan

Native Language: English

Favorite Food: Onigiri

Favorite Activity: Playing

Favorite Bible Verse: "The LORD is indeed going before you—he will be with you; he will not fail you or abandon you. Do not be afraid or discouraged!" (Deuteronomy 31:8). Find Natalie's artwork on page 42.

Nathalia

Country: France
Native Languages: Spanish and French
Favorite Food: Croque monsieur
Favorite Activity: Coloring
Favorite Bible Verse: "The LORD is my shepherd, I lack nothing" (Psalm 23:1). Find Nathalia's artwork on page 146.

Nathaniel

Country: Greece
Native Language: Greek
Favorite Foods: Lentil soup and milk pie
Favorite Activity: Playing with LEGOs
Favorite Bible Verse: "Don't be afraid, for I am with you! Don't be frightened, for I am your God! I strengthen you—yes, I help you—yes, I uphold you with my victorious right hand!" (Isaiah 41:10). Find Nathaniel's artwork on page 21.

Nehemiah

Country: Thailand
Native Language: English
Favorite Food: Bacon
Favorite Activity: Playing soccer
Favorite Bible Verse: "Create for me a pure heart, O God. Renew a resolute spirit within me" (Psalm 51:10). Find Nehemiah's artwork on page 77.

Nolan

Country: United States of America
Native Language: English
Favorite Food: Pizza
Favorite Bible Verse: "I am able to do all things through the one who strengthens me" (Philippians 4:13). Find Nolan's artwork on page 140.

Richard

Country: Uganda
Native Language: Luganda
Favorite Food: Matooke and chicken
Favorite Bible Verse: "But Jesus said, 'Let the little children come to me and do not try to stop them, for the kingdom of heaven belongs to such as these'" (Matthew 19:14). Find Richard's artwork on page 48.

Rose

Country: Northern Ireland
Native Language: English
Favorite Activity: Listening to music
Favorite Bible Verse: "He says, 'Stop your striving and recognize that I am God. I will be exalted over the nations! I will be exalted over the earth!'" (Psalm 46:10). Find Rose's artwork on page 192.

Simão

Country: Portugal
Native Language: Portuguese
Favorite Food: Seafood rice
Favorite Bible Verse: "I was glad because they said to me, 'We will go to the LORD's temple'" (Psalm 122:1). Find Simão's artwork on page 58.

Sofia

Country: Slovakia
Native Language: Slovak
Favorite Food: Sheep cheese gnocchi
Favorite Activity: Reading
Favorite Bible Verse: "The LORD strengthens and protects me; I trust in him with all my heart. I am rescued and my heart is full of joy; I will sing to him in gratitude" (Psalm 28:7).
Find Sofia's artwork on page 159.

Thanat Jade

Country: Thailand
Native Language: Thai
Favorite Food: Barbecue pork with sticky rice
Favorite Activities: Drawing and coloring
Favorite Bible Verse: "Trust in the LORD with all your heart, and do not rely on your own understanding. Acknowledge him in all your ways, and he will make your paths straight" (Proverbs 3:5–6).
Find Thanat Jade's artwork on page 46.

Yoshiya

Country: Japan
Native Language: English
Favorite Foods: Ice cream, pudding, and sweet oranges
Favorite Activities: Riding bicycles, playing with LEGOs, and playing board games
Favorite Bible Verse: "A gentle response turns away anger, but a harsh word stirs up wrath" (Proverbs 15:1).
Find Yoshiya's artwork on page 178.

Zawadi

Country: Kenya
Native Language: Swahili
Favorite Food: Ugali and fish
Favorite Bible Verse: "For this is the way God loved the world: He gave his one and only Son, so that everyone who believes in him will not perish but have eternal life" (John 3:16).
Find Zawadi's artwork on page 92.

Zoé

Country: The Netherlands
Native Language: Dutch
Favorite Food: Pizza
Favorite Activity: Reading
Favorite Bible Verse: "Arise! Shine! For your light arrives! The splendor of the LORD shines on you!" (Isaiah 60:1).
Find Zoé's artwork on page 29.